The Changing Structure of British Foreign Policy

The Changing Structure of British Foreign Policy

ROY E. JONES

Longman

Longman
1724-1974

LONGMAN GROUP LTD, London
and LONGMAN INC. New York

*Associated companies, branches and representatives
throughout the world*

First published 1974

ISBN 0 582 50710 3
Library of Congress Catalog Card Number 73-94031

Set in Bembo (220) 11/12 pt
and printed in Great Britain
by Butler & Tanner Ltd, Frome and London

Contents

Introduction: Foreign policy   1

Part One   SETTINGS

1 The strategic habitat   17
2 The economic habitat   35
3 The institutional habitat   54

Part Two   THE BRITISH SITUATION

4 The strategic predicament   69
5 The economic predicament   92
6 The institutional predicament   109

Part Three   THE VOCABULARY OF FOREIGN POLICY

7 Power   123
8 Democracy   140
9 Control   165
10 The changing structure of British foreign policy   179

Further Reading   182

Index   187

Introduction: Foreign policy

WHAT IS FOREIGN POLICY?

Common usage establishes a straightforward notion of what foreign policy is: the actions and purposes of the state in the world beyond its own territorial boundaries. The foreign policy of Britain is what this state does, and what it intends by those actions, beyond the shores of the British Isles. This usage is embedded in the assumption that the physical position and resources of these islands, together with the values of British society, constitute an historically consistent discipline on the state in its overseas operations. Equally, it is assumed that the state in its dealings abroad is confronted by a hazardous, unstable and potentially hostile environment which has rigours of its own. Here the state must beware of wishful thinking about the intentions of other states with different interests and values. In its foreign actions the state must therefore be primarily guided by the national interest of Britain and must be supremely cautious in matters risking the safety, welfare and political equilibrium of British society. Though it may bear international testimony to the values of British society, it must not endanger stability at home through the assumption of overseas obligations, duties or hostilities which it has not the strength or conviction to sustain.

This doctrine of foreign policy emphasises three forms of reality: the structural dominance of the state, the distinction between the domestic and the international aspects of politics, and the priority of the national interest.

QUALIFICATIONS

This is a doctrine which appears to be straightforward and practical. It may also be one which is widely held to be true among statesmen and diplomatists. But it is open to a number of simple criticisms.

1. It equates the British state with the British political system. The state is Britain in the international arena.

This position must mean either that the state is all political relations in Britain, or that the state dominates political relations in Britain. If the state is political relations in Britain then it must be equated with all the legal institutions of British political life, local and national; with all the groups of British politics; with all relations between these groups, and between these groups and legal institutions; and it must be equated with all the arguments of British politics. If all this is so, then it follows that the state, among other things, is a large number of continuing conflicts between groups and institutions about what their relations are or should be. It follows that for an observer in Britain the state must be so complex, so full of internal contradictions, as to defy clear perception or determinate description. If this is so, how can the same observer distinguish the state as a simple and coherent entity, as a single actor, in international relations?

If the state is not the totality of British political relations but something which is pre-eminent among them, then it must be distinguishable in terms of usage (something which is commonly described and understood to be the state), or in terms of its distinctive quality (its superior power or influence). In common usage the term most often occurs in connection with symbols ('state ceremonies') and in connection with machinery of public administration ('welfare state'). If the state is a symbol then there is little meaning in saying that the state acts externally, since the acts of a symbol must themselves be symbolic. If the state is an administrative mechanism then it is equally difficult to see what the foreign actions of the state can be taken to refer to, since, in broad terms, British administrative mechanisms do not operate widely overseas.

If the state is taken to be something which is distinctive, and distinctively important, because of its pre-eminent power then its essential site should be clearly visible. The body or institution with most power over men should be detectable as the source of the orders and prohibitions which they obey. Yet generations of constitutional and political commentators have been at odds in their discoveries of this essential centre of power in Britain. The electorate, an elite, political parties, the House of Commons, the bureaucracy, the Cabinet, the person and office of Prime Minister have all been plausibly identified. As well, power has been found to be distributed differently at different periods and in relation to different issues. The effect of pursuits and discoveries such as these is that power dissolves among the disparate components of British politics, its groups, institutions, laws, practices and personalities. The state-as-power is overwhelmed by politics.

2. The traditional doctrine of foreign policy makes an emphatic distinction between the internal relations of the state and the external relations of the state, between domestic politics and international politics. This distinction is of central importance for two reasons. First, it is implied that the confusions inherent in the notion of the state as the prime actor in the domestic arena disappear when the state is described from the standpoint of the international arena. Second, it is also implied that the actions of the state take on a determinate nature (become distinctive as foreign policy) because the dangers of the international environment are such as to compel it to act according to an externally determined pattern which is common to all states. In terms of an image as old as the notion of the state itself, the hazards of the oceans are so compelling that a given ship, whatever its internal social arrangements and customs, must be handled along lines common to all ships if it is to avoid disaster.

The peculiar character of the international arena is often held to reside in three prominent and closely related qualities. First, in the international arena the control of the legitimate exercise of physical force is diffused among states, not concentrated as it is within a given state. Second, actors in the international arena do not move within a legal order, whereas inside the state the actions of men, groups and institutions are controlled by such an order. Third, at the international level there is a high measure of uncertainty as to the location of the power of decision and this is not the case for issues confronting men at the domestic level.

It would be folly to deny the existence of any sense of reality in these perceptions. But their clarity is not self-evident. The argument which concentrates on the diffused nature of the control and use of force at the international level is suspect, particularly when used in relation to a second-class power such as Britain. The supreme capability to exercise international force is not diffused but concentrated in the hands of the governments of the Soviet Union and the United States, and these two governments are bound in a deterrence relationship which is absorbed in the non-use, not the use, of large-scale violence. In Britain's immediate vicinity in Europe there are a number of military forces comparable to her own. To suggest that these forces are at the clear disposition of individual governments is to distort reality. These governments are not capable of going to war in their continental setting; except, possibly, against one another, and this they show no inclination to do.

The existence of national military forces is not to be confused with their use, or in a large number of cases, with distinct threats of their use.

Similarly, the idea that at the domestic level large-scale force is concentrated in governmental hands is too simple to withstand examination. It is a longstanding scholastic dogma that the distinctive feature of internal political activity is that it is concerned with making decisions for the national society behind which lies the threat of the legitimate use of force. But if Britain is a political society (not, say, a dictatorial society) then it follows that large-scale decisions are the result of pressures, arguments, negotiations, alliances and compromises. If this is so it must follow that political decisions are acceptable because they are made politically, not because they are supported by the sanction of force. Concentration of the control of force is therefore substantially an irrelevance to power in domestic decisions. The notion that force is concentrated, not diffused, at the international level, but diffused, not concentrated, at the domestic level, might therefore be plausibly held to be as true as the converse. If two opposing statements seem to be true, then a strong indication is conveyed that the underlying phenomena to which they are applied are too complex to be described by either of them.

The idea that a legal order exists at the national level and does not exist at the international level is similarly unsubtle. At the international level governments certainly make agreements with one another. A characteristic of these agreements is not that they are all neglected and abandoned, but that most of them are not neglected and abandoned. An important aspect of a legal order is the habit and agreement of its members in proceeding politically in making their agreements and in enacting regulations. The legal order in Britain may be conceived in part as a set of working adjustments between the forces of British society (trade unions, industrialists, religions, professions and so on). In this sense, legal orders undoubtedly exist in international society; in Western Europe, for example, or in the Western international economy. Even at the highest level of international conflict, the nuclear deterrence system, there is a certain consensus among the powers most strenuously engaged as to the manner in which agreements should be reached and the lengths to which disagreements should be taken. The notion of legal orders at the international level is not a simple and clear one. Nor can it be denied that international legal orders are cumbrous entities, slow to produce clear regulations. But this is not to concede that international relations are sharply divided from domestic relations by their lack of the framework of legal order.

Thirdly, it is by no means indisputable that a distinctive quality of the international arena is the uncertainty it engenders about the location of authority. At the domestic level legitimate authority is not a precise, clearly placed quantity. In a pluralist society such as Britain's, it is by no means always easy to predict the kinds of regulations to which powerful groups and institutions will agree. To say that the British government has authority is to say very little; much depends on the issues with which it is confronted. The legislative process in Britain might be described as a system whereby sets of diplomatic negotiations are conducted among the powers of British society. At the international level, the location of authority in relation to particular issues is sometimes quite clear. There can be little doubt, for example, that the regulation of nuclear armaments is primarily, though not wholly, a matter for the first-rank powers. Similarly, the regulation of the Western international monetary system is primarily a matter for the governments of the Western industrialised countries. Reaching agreement at the international level can be laborious. But it can sometimes be equally laborious at the national level.

If a fully determinate distinction between the nature of the internal relations of the state and the external relations of the state cannot be made, it follows that a determinate conception of the state in an international environment of other states ceases to be a realistic foundation of an understanding of foreign policy.

3. Associated with the traditional distinction between the nature of the external political setting and the nature of the internal political setting is the notion of the impermeability of state boundaries. Impermeability is also a concomitant of the assumption that external relations take the form of a single channel of influence and communication which is dominated by the state and its diplomatic agents. The state, in this general view, is connected with the international setting by a specific channel and what the state and its agents do and say in this channel constitutes foreign policy.

The impermeability of state boundaries may be questioned on a large number of practical and conceptual grounds. Most elementarily, the boundaries of Britain are not impermeable to disease and environmental pollutions; to radio communications; to opinions, beliefs, fashions and, more important, scientific knowledge; to attack by nuclear missiles or to the effects of nuclear detonations elsewhere. Many individual citizens travel, communicate and form associations in disregard of national boundaries. Trade and transnational movements of capital affect their lives. Many citizens find employment in companies whose owners and principal managers are not British. Large numbers of transnational organisations, most obviously the apparatus of the European Community, have a direct impact within British territory. Similarly, many British organisations conduct their own brand of foreign relations: trade unions, political parties, private companies and the like, operate policies of their own in relation to similar structures abroad, to governmental authorities abroad, and in relation to transnational markets in goods, capital and enterprise.

This extensive range of international activities is complemented by an almost equally complex governmental involvement overseas. Almost all government departments have close links with foreign counterparts through transnational organisations, and almost all government ministers participate in international gatherings of some kind. Many parliamentarians are active in international assemblies of formal or informal kinds. Almost all the principal elements of the British political system are active both domestically and internationally. Additionally, state diplomacy guided by state foreign policy has itself negotiated British entry into transnational organisations which themselves complicate notions of the state. Nato, for example, exercises a degree of authority over the most central traditional international token and instrument of the state, its armed forces. The organs of the European Community are involved in many aspects of government regulation of commercial and industrial life; they promulgate regulations having direct authority within British frontiers; and they even have a direct impact on the most traditionally sensitive of political issues, the distribution of public expenditure.

No view of foreign policy which assumes impermeability of national society can adequately explain actions of foreign policy which increase its permeability.

4. If one accepts the concept of the impermeable state as the irreducible reality of global politics, then it might seem true that government is confronted by a simple field of action in the international arena. States are identical in nature, though not in strength. From time to time they collide, rarely head-on but often obliquely, and when they do so their

paths are altered in ways strictly determined by their relative size and impetus. They may link themselves in alliances to pursue joint ends which seem likely to yield a more substantial return to partners than each could individually acquire. They may join together to secure their defences in times of mutual danger. But alliances do not alter the units which form them. When objectives are achieved, the spoils are shared according to the relative strengths and bargaining skills of erstwhile allies. When danger has passed, partners in defence go their separate ways, to re-form in different configurations as new hazards appear.

In a world like this there is such a thing as an entirely separate and coherent foreign policy, and its objectives, as distinct from its tactics, may be very simple: to maintain the independent existence of the state, to preserve and increase its possessions, to spare it material loss, to secure for it material gain, to see that it is on the winning side in any conflict, to keep a watchful eye on its competitors (that is, on all other states) and to be on guard against placing it in a position of dependence on any one of them. In these endeavours the statesman must maintain a cool and realistic view of the capabilities of his own state in relation to those of other states, and must never allow himself to be moved by sentiment or by an over-scrupulous observance in his statecraft of those moral rules which he may value in his private life. In summary, he maintains, pursues, and is guided by, the national interest.

Given the permeable nature of the national political system, the imprecision of the notion of the state and the absence of an impregnable barrier between domestic and international forms of politics, the strictly national interest may often be transformed into a general concern with the total environment, both national and international, of the functions of government. Governments often struggle with common transnational problems, and though their interests may not be identical their associations may go far beyond anything which might reasonably be described as temporary conjunctions of states pursuing specific ends. For example, the governments of the principal Western countries are almost constantly engaged with the problem of order in the international monetary system. This intricate task does not comprise an alliance in any ordinary sense. It is a joint political-economic enterprise of indefinite duration, which is transnational in terms of the phenomenon to which it is addressed, in terms of the informed discourse attaching to those phenomena, and in terms of the impact of any regulatory outcomes which may prove practicable. Not merely are governments engaged in transnational enterprises such as this, the environment in which they pursue interests may be of such a nature as to weaken the distinctions upon which the idea of the priority of the wholly national interest depends. The pursuit of prosperity and the pursuit of international influence, in Europe and elsewhere, led a British government to join the European Community, but the European Community's programme is one which undermines the meaning of national integrity.

Similarly, if a government is but one element in the national political system, and if the global field of relations in which it operates is a far from simple one, it follows that a claim by it that in specific issues it is guided by the interest of a national society is one which must almost always be a source of intense political dispute. If it is disputed it cannot be national. In a plural society, exact knowledge of the national interest cannot be claimed in either domestic or international circumstances except where an issue creates a massive political consensus. But even in this event, actions taken in the context of a consensus may subsequently be judged to have been harmful and the consensus in question to have been based on an illusion, as is a common contemporary view of Britain's involvement in the Munich agreement of 1938. In the more mundane context of the present settlement in Europe, the national interest conceived as both the central fact of foreign policy and as the sole reliable guide of statesmen, fails to come alive in the context, for example, of Community discussions about the regulation of maximum axle-weights of trucks which may be permitted to operate on European roads. In an issue such as this, large numbers of groups and institutions express themselves—haulage companies, trading companies, conservation groups, ancient municipalities, even churches. Here there is no clear national interest, but a mass of contending interests, some expressed nationally, others expressed transnationally.

5. The specific elements of the traditional doctrine of foreign policy are questionable. Its general intellectual stance is also the subject of fundamental objection.

Essentially, the traditional doctrine of foreign policy represents a static view of international relations. This is so because it assumes that the state is the perpetually dominant unit of international action. On the international stage there is only one role, the role of the state, and the only element of variety is provided by this role being played by large, medium and small actors of uneven competence. If the traditional doctrine of foreign policy is true, it follows that there can be no fundamental transformation in global relations. All change occurs within a fixed frame of reference: some states rise, others decline, alliances form, then dissolve. Within this rigid frame there is a great deal of activity but nothing happens.

The static nature of the traditional doctrine may be questioned in two fundamental ways. First, if it assumes that what it refers to is changeless then it is wrong, and the kinds of actions it recommends must also, at some time, be wrong. Explaining phenomena which are assumed never to change is easy; explaining the transformation of phenomena is far more difficult; explaining changing phenomena as if they were changeless is dangerous. The only transformation which the traditional doctrine might explain is the transformation produced by miscalculations of national interests resulting in general holocaust. An explanation goes some way towards encompassing the possibilities of transformation when it is seen merely as a special explanation set within a framework which is acknowledged to be limited. The traditional doctrine of foreign policy rarely conveys this sense of modesty.

Second, a doctrine which would confine men within changeless conceptual walls would also blind them to possibilities of moral and intellectual growth offered by the wider environment. The inaccuracy of such a doctrine is the lesser of its defects: it is also morally wrong.

6. The emphasis of the traditional doctrine clearly falls on foreign policy as the practice of 'high' statecraft. The collisions and alignments of states comprise the material of foreign policy and inherent in this material is the possibility of massive violence.

This bias of the traditional doctrine distracts attention from a prominent modern transformation in foreign relations, which is the massively increased presence there of matters of 'low' policy. The arrangement of international credits, abstruse discussions about monetary reforms, attempts to organise or regulate transnational industrial and scientific projects, concern about the policies of particular transnational companies, repetitive and heated debates about related agricultural policies, attempts to cope with large speculative movements of capital: these are the kinds of items to which a substantial measure of governmental activity, and public attention, is commonly addressed. 'Low' foreign policy absorbs governments fully, raises sensitive questions of domestic politics, but does not occupy the 'high' international stage, where issues of peace and war, the rise and fall of nations, are the traditional dramatic themes. Yet 'low' foreign policy frequently calls into question both the practical relevance of national boundaries and the power of individual governments to regulate such mundane matters as domestic rates of interest, when these are elements in transnational systems. 'Low' policy is often concerned with international entities other than states, with multinational companies, transnational markets, pollutions of the environment and suchlike. Statehood is not irrelevant to these concerns, but it commands something less than a monopoly of influence over them.

WIDER ASSUMPTIONS

If men widely adhere to a doctrine, then it must have some truth as a means of explaining their actions and their expectations. The gravamen of the criticisms of the traditional doctrine of foreign policy mentioned above is not that this doctrine is trivial or without operational effect, since it is neither, but that its parameters are limited and that, consequently, it coherently describes only a segment of the data of foreign relations. It is essentially a special and not a general interpretation of those relations.

Treating the traditional doctrine as a special interpretation does not require the invention of a more general theory of international relations, which would take the form of an even more grandiose doctrine. This form of social alchemy is avoided in this essay by a strategy based on four sets of assumptions.

1. Global relations are taken to be a field and not a system. To put specific systemic boundaries to this field is taken to be as distorting as, say, to attempt to put physical boundaries round the concept of space in theoretical physics. The impulses which comprise the field of global relations are taken to be ideas, doctrines and actions. Specific sets of these relations (ideas, doctrines, and actions relating to the balance of power, for example) can be partially described. But there can be no general explanation of the field as a whole. This is so for three basic reasons: first, a general theory must immediately become a part of the field, subject to its forces, and cannot transcend it in any

sense: second, because the field has no boundaries it cannot be distinguished from something else and it cannot, even conceptually, be observed or analysed from outside; third, the forces of the field must together be more complex than the human mind (engendering, as they do, the categories and notions comprising the human mind) and the mind cannot reduce to generalities something which is more complex than itself.

2. Within the field of global relations, systems of actions and ideas are taken to be distinguishable; but the boundaries of these systems are taken to be highly imperfect in the context of the field as a whole. The imperfection of boundaries means: first, that though much can be said about a given system such as the balance of power (which can, as it were, be observed from an external standpoint), any attempt at a complete explanation must assume entirely coherent boundaries and thus distort reality to the point of constructing an artificial model of it; and, second, that a given system is subject to transforming forces which cannot all be incorporated into the terms of the system's explanation. Thus a balance of power system, which includes the orientations of participants towards the balance of power, can be distinguished and its workings analysed in terms of the number of states in the system, the number of possible combinations between them, and the possibilities of disequilibrium, or even breakdown, resulting from these combinations. But the system may be transformed by forces which cannot be placed within its boundaries or incorporated into its languages: by religion, or ideology, or technical advance.

In the nature of the field of global relations, the systems which can be distinguished within it overlap and relate in the most complex ways. The system of independent sovereign states can be distinguished (with all the dogma attaching to it); the system of nuclear deterrence can also be distinguished (and it includes ideas about, and governmental orientations towards, nuclear deterrence); and the Western international monetary system can similarly be distinguished (which also proliferates ideas about itself). These systems do not coincide: the system of sovereign independent states is not the same as the nuclear deterrence system, if only because the latter renders some states distinctly less than sovereign in their pursuit of defence. There are no absolute boundaries between these systems: the problems of the Western monetary system are partly created by different uses of sovereignty by different states; the availability of armaments is related to the mobilisation of economic resources; and the strategies of military forces in Nato are related by governments to problems within the Western monetary system.

3. There are discontinuities within the field of global relations, but no discontinuity is taken to be complete. Different kinds of discontinuities rarely coincide exactly. And the discontinuities associated with the concept of the state are extremely variable.

A discontinuity between rich and poor countries can be distinguished; but it is not a clear one (China is a poor but also a powerful country, and a number of oil-producers, though industrially underdeveloped, are very rich), and large numbers of systems contain both rich and poor countries (the international trade system, for example). A discontinuity between the communist and liberal value systems can be distinguished; but it is not a clear one (where can Czechoslovakia be placed in ideological terms?) and major parties on both sides of the divide are intimately related in other systems (most notably in the system of nuclear deterrence). The discontinuities between first-rank powers and lesser powers are very marked in relation to some systems (nuclear deterrence again) but not so marked in relation to others (as in the case of the United States in relation to other rich countries in the international monetary system). And the discontinuities marked by state boundaries do not dominate other kinds of continuities (the discontinuity in the matter of immigration into Britain does not dictate a similar discontinuity in the movement of goods and capital).

4. Governments, rather than states, are taken to be particularly evident in the international arena, but they do not necessarily dominate it. There are other actors, such as multinational companies. And some systems in which governments are involved have a coherent presence of such force that an individual government may scarcely seem to be an actor at all: again the nuclear deterrence system is an appropriate example. Some systems, as it were, call the tune to governments: the transnational system of the physical sciences has an impact which few governments can resist. The actions of governments towards one another often refer not to the prosecution of their immediate interests but to the management of transnational systems: thus recurrent efforts are made to achieve the governability of the Western international monetary system.

The notion of governments as principal, but not necessarily wholly dominant, international actors is a more flexible one than the notion of states-as-actors. Governments vary in their capabilities almost on a day-to-day basis, depending on the issues confronting them and the forces at play in those issues. The notion of sovereignty has no such built-in variability. A government conducting relations with another government takes account of the effects of different personalities and differing domestic political circumstances. Governments have a human dimension of adaptability, weakness and fallibility lacking in the notion of the state. Also governments may change their interpretation of their interests in a short space of time. The state and the national interest have a timeless quality at odds with the shifting world of practical experience.

The explanatory apparatus of the traditional doctrine of foreign policy can still be applied to the British case. But the profound penetrations of the national political system, the efforts of governments to enter into the regulation of systems of action which do not conform to national boundaries, the existence of transnational organisations of a variety of kinds, the variability of national and transnational boundaries, these and other factors undermine the categories inherent in the traditional framework. What follows addresses itself to some of the principal problems, both hazardous and creative in their implications, raised by this changing structure of foreign policy.

Part One   Settings

1 The strategic habitat

GOVERNMENT AND SECURITY

A government concerned for safety has a range of conceivable policies before it. At one extreme of this range it may opt for pure defence, building up its own strength so that it can take on all comers. At the other it may abandon all defences and alliances and commit itself to world security through the establishment of an organised world order. At one pole the sovereignty of the state is all-important, at the other it is substantially abandoned.

The prospect of life at either of these poles is seldom to the liking of most governments. A country relying on pure defence washes its hands of world security and relies on its own strength and on its geographical situation to keep it from direct attack, and from the destructive effects of quarrels among other powers. Such a country must be supremely confident of its strength to defend itself, or in its intrinsic capacity to keep out of international disorders.

In the thermonuclear age all countries are exposed to the possibility of military attack and the best that can be achieved by way of pure nuclear defence is to threaten a possible opponent with a punishing riposte should an attack be launched. This is the policy of deterrence. Its essential characteristic is that it aims to create a psychological climate in which the danger of an attack is reduced. By definition the deterrer is drawn into the deterrence relationship. He will be concerned to make this relationship a stable one, for instability is likely to destroy his safety. In this kind of way the deterrer is propelled towards a concern with the conditions of international security. The core of nuclear deterrence must lie in the relations between the principal deterrers, the first-class powers, whose strategic weapons are most likely to survive an all-out attack from any source. Yet because a breakdown of deterrence could have a catastrophic consequence for the world at large, all other powers, particularly those closely connected by alliance or geography with the first-rankers, have a central interest in stable deterence. There is, then, an elementary world security interest.

But complete dedication to world security, involving the neglect of individual or collective defence, is not an attractive policy for individual governments concerned about national safety. By definition a government adhering to such a policy submerges itself completely in the world arena and in attempts to render it orderly and secure. A moment's contemplation of this prospect reveals difficulties of formidable scope. Involvement in the world means involvement in the world's quarrels, and these are not always amenable to solution through rational investigation, deliberation and compromise. If a world order in a complete form were instituted it would need machinery to discipline deviant governments. It would need central direction and a military capability sufficient to control any national government or combination of national governments.

Such a leap to the realisation of absolute world security may seem undesirable on the ground that a supremely powerful world authority could too easily become a supremely powerful world tyranny. There are more immediately persuasive practical objections; a world government could not acquire overwhelming military force overnight, and in the lengthy interim could itself be deterred by national nuclear forces; national governments would not surrender military strength to a central world authority unless they trusted one another, but it is because they do not wholly trust one another that they possess military forces in the first place; given the precedents of the League of Nations and the United Nations, the world authority could not be expected to be always given to rapid and firm decision, but an irresolute world authority would not be authoritative and would not be trusted to provide world security.

Absolute security through world organisation seems to be no more attainable than absolute defence through national strength and alliances of national strengths. Thus governments struggle with the problem of achieving safety through the pursuit of imperfect defence and imperfect international security. These two elements are commonly embedded in their strategic policies, where they create tensions familiar to the practical world of politics. The central problem of foreign policy within the strategic habitat lies in synthesising these two elements.

THE CURRENT DIMENSIONS OF MILITARY STRENGTH

The most fundamental feature of the strategic setting in which British governments find themselve is the large gap which exists between the military strength of first-rank states and the military strength of lesser states. The extent of this discontinuity is unexampled since the decline of Imperial Rome. It is associated with a pace of technical change so great and costly that only a first-rank power can match the military strength of another first-rank power. It is also the case that no combination of lesser states can place itself on the military level of the first-rank powers through a traditional alliance. Though it may be conceivable that lesser states could pool their resources to a degree sufficient to provide the required scale of military investment and to achieve the unity of command without which sufficient resources cannot be effectively deployed, integration taken to this level means the creation of a new first-rank state, and the creation of an entirely new state is a massive social and political enterprise.

Alternatively, a lesser government, such as that of Japan, might resolve to raise itself to the first rank. But a modern armoury is immensely expensive. For a lesser state, even one as wealthy as Japan, to mobilise resources on this scale, its government would have to feel it to be in imminent danger of attack. During the present period of strategic stalemate among existing first-rank states this required sense of intense local danger appears to be absent. The route to the first rank is thus intimidatingly complex and demanding. Yet a simple combination of essentially similar second-rank forces is not now convincing at the first-rank level, as might have been the case before the introduction of nuclear weapons.

Since the Second World War nationalism has prospered and the form of the state proliferates as never before. Among new states deficiencies in economic endowment and political stability are very evident. Internal political instability and disorder are endemic in large areas of the world. Opportunities for intervention by outside powers sometimes appear to be great. But war inside the territories and societies of other states has become a formidably more political activity than the European colonial excursions of the past. The outcome of modern 'sub-limited' wars of this internal kind can bear very little relation to the military strength of interventionists. Apparently straightforward support for a friendly government becomes formidably complex when that government's legitimacy is questioned.

Despite the high level of international and subnational tensions, and the large number of vehement actors in the international arena, the actual level of sustained violence is low in relation to the total abundance of technical means of destruction. This is so partly because of the reluctance of the first-rank states to engage in direct mutual hostilities. If one first-rank power is involved in a local war (in Korea or Vietnam or Hungary) the other avoids a similarly direct intervention. Also, the former first-rank states of Europe are no longer disposed to fight one another. Their empires have almost totally dissolved and they lack the means and the will to engage wholeheartedly in overseas expeditions. Along with the United States they recognise, and for practical purposes accept, the existence of a Soviet empire in Eastern Europe and do not attempt to challenge Soviet military actions there. In an age of extremely rapid mass politicisation, notions of justice figure prominently in the rhetoric of world politics: but in Europe and elsewhere men are sometimes prepared to settle for what is ordered rather than for what they claim to be right. Among other factors, the common acceptance of the form of the state, even in areas where its practical reality may be dubious tends towards the effect of preventing the spread of internal violence beyond national boundaries: so far the level of violence within African states has been in no way matched by the level of violence between African states. And, where they occur (in the Middle East or in the Indian subcontinent, for example), international hostilities are contained at a regional level, largely because it is in nobody's interest to see a local international war raised to a potentially catastrophic world level of violence.

The central fact of strategy for European governments such as those of Britain is the massive concentration of nuclear weapons in the hands of the United States and the Soviet Union and of the close involvement of both these powers in Europe. Large numbers of nuclear weapons controlled by these two governments are deployed in Europe, and there are numbers of nuclear weapons deployed outside Europe which have European targets. Thus far, the situation is only slightly complicated by the small nuclear capabilities of the governments of Britain and France. British governments are dependent on the United States for the provision of essential elements of their more advanced weapons. Beneath the nuclear canopy large standing armies are stationed in Europe, and by far the weightier of these are controlled by the government of the Soviet Union.

No state below the first rank can receive a determined major attack from a first-ranker and still retaliate on a like scale. This is not to suggest that the governments of the United States and the Soviet Union can impose their wills all over the world with the ease with which they could deliver thermonuclear devastation. This is clearly not so. Most obviously these powers limit each other. They create formidable risks for each other wherever their foreign policies meet. Nuclear pressure is not influential where nuclear attack, though technically possible, is not likely to occur. Partly for ideological reasons, partly because of the fear of triggering a central nuclear conflict, and partly because of the sheer pointlessness of creating contaminated wastelands of no strategic or political value, neither of the first-rank governments is inclined to use its strategic weapons in underdeveloped areas. A first-rank interest in a regional interstate conflict (such as that between India and Pakistan) is commonly furthered by supporting one or the other of the parties on a fairly modest scale. In the case of armed conflict within a state, an interested outsider must weigh the merits of various forms of involvement, from the quasidiplomatic to the military. If intervention does take place, non-nuclear means are favoured, and, dependent upon indigenous political conditions, these may be inadequate to the tasks in hand. Minor nuclear powers are even less likely to use nuclear strength in third areas than the major nuclear states, since this would inevitably incur the practical displeasure of first-rankers anxious to avoid their own mutual involvement in a nuclear outburst initiated by another government. Similarly, non-nuclear intervention by minor nuclear powers is inhibited by the factors weighing upon major powers and by the additional factor of more limited strength and heavier dependence on allies, both local and otherwise.

Because nuclear weapons are capable of bringing calamitous consequences to their users they are deployed in the service of policies of deterrence. This policy, though it has complex forms, is almost always one of presenting an opponent with threats so formidably convincing as to circumscribe any intention he may have of orthodox military advance. The effect of threats is the creation of risks, and the essential nature of risk is psychological. One can never be certain that one's own threat is going to have the desired effect, and one's opponent can never be certain that one would actually perform the threatened action if put to the test. Nuclear threats create risks of injury of the most formidable kind. These are shared by the principal nuclear powers and by the world at large. The scale of risks produces a common concern on the part of the principals to maximise control of nuclear weapons and minimise the possibilities of nuclear detonation being caused by miscalculation, accident, or the irresponsibility of third parties. Policies of nuclear deterrence do not exist within the context of purely conflict relationship; they create cooperative interests which the principals pursue both formally and informally.

In broad terms the purpose of nuclear weapons is negative, to prevent advances, not positive, to further advances. Even in this negative function their effectiveness is limited. Their existence may help to prevent a Soviet nuclear intrusion into the Caribbean by way of Cuba; but they cannot prevent an unwelcome change in the nature of Cuban government and politics. Though they might be used effectively against modern armies in a continental context, their relevance to the destruction of subversive forces operating among large populations in underdeveloped areas is remote.

The bipolarity of the international strategic system is thus complicated by the obvious fact that vast nuclear strength does not yield effective power to alter the course of events in many parts of the world. Yet it would be folly to conclude on this evidence that strategic bipolarity is illusory. One must assume that the first-rank governments would use nuclear weapons, not necessarily indiscriminately, if they felt their core interests and values to be at stake. Their core interests and values are self-determined. For British governments there are thus two fundamental areas of uncertainty, created by the two dimensions, conflict and cooperation, of deterrence: first, the degree and form of cooperation which is desirable and attainable among the first-rank powers and its possible consequences for Britain and Europe; and, second, the strength of the United States commitment to her allies in the context of great power conflict.

Europe is not an underdeveloped area containing a large peasant population where subversionary warfare is likely to yield substantial political results. It is a wealthy land mass containing a number of complicated territorial and political boundaries, where continental armies are deployed, where nuclear weapons of various potentialities are thickly sited, and where the spheres of interest of the first-rank powers meet more directly than in almost any other part of the world. It is sheathed by seas where large naval forces, also armed with nuclear weapons, constantly manœuvre and patrol. Britain is permanently anchored on the edge of this continent and her security policies are profoundly affected by the military facts of her situation. Her governments must be concerned that Western European countries with governments of friendly disposition are not overrun or pressured into hostile policies. British governments must additionally be concerned with political configurations between the first-class powers, between the first-rank powers and the European theatre generally, and between the lesser European powers themselves. The search for safety in this setting led Britain to be a prominent founding member of both an early postwar military alliance among Western European countries, and, later, of the larger alliance which links the United States with Western Europe in Nato.

In the past Britain's strategic emphasis on Europe has been distracted by the fact that Britain emerged from the Second World War in the guise of a victorious world power of the first rank. Her colonial and Commonwealth attachments, her extensive overseas economic interests and involvements, and her widely used currency commanded much of the attention of British governments. The dissolution of the Empire, the weakening of the Commonwealth, the failure of the anachronistic expedition on Suez, and the apparently insuperable political difficulty of allocating greater elements of public expenditure to the maintenance of large overseas forces, have tended to sharpen strategic attention to Europe and to the conjunction of first-rank policies as they affect Europe. Yet small British military forces remain deployed outside the European theatre, most notably in Singapore and the Indian Ocean. In any large-scale conflict, within or between states, forces such as these are of questionable military or political value. In themselves they are unlikely to determine a large-scale outcome, but British governments are unlikely ever to be in a position to reinforce them substantially. They could only be effective in conjunction with larger military commitments from other quarters, either indigenous or external. There are very few indigenous governments (in the Persian Gulf or in East Africa, for example) which regard the possibility of British military intervention in any form as desirable. Externally, the United States is the only power currently capable of supporting Britain on a large military scale. But the future military role of the United States in the underdeveloped countries is far from clear. For the reasons indicated, American governments have experienced a contraction in their sense of military power. This is not to argue that there can be no role whatever for British forces outside Europe, but it is to argue that whatever role is suggested must be a very discreet and subtle one.

EUROPE AND THE FIRST-CLASS POWERS

The two first-rank powers are locked in a relationship which emphasises both cooperation and conflict. These two intricately related themes
of deterrence intimately affect the strategic future of Britain and Europe.
In the early years of the nuclear age the strategic policy of the United
States was, or seemed to be, the simple one of massive retaliation. An
advance by the Soviet Union would be met by an all-out counterattack
by the United States in support of, and supported by, her allies. Reflection on this policy in the United States and among her allies, the
development of thermonuclear weapons of horrific strength, and the
rapid acquisition by the Soviet Union of a complete nuclear and missile
armoury, combined to reveal its defects. A fixed commitment to expand
a minor military incident, if such were to occur in Europe, into a
spasm of nuclear devastation, was not a policy which could withstand
rational analysis for long. Massive retaliation represented a determination to abandon political control of violence in times of utmost crisis.
Yet it would be at times of utmost crisis that the world, and the allies,
would stand most in need of political control and creativity. It was also
the case that massive retaliation would certainly devastate the area in
which the triggering incident took place. The countries of Western
Europe could not contemplate this prospect with equanimity. Additionally, as Soviet capabilities increased, it became clear that massive
retaliation could bring the riposte of nuclear bombardment from the
Soviet Union to the homeland of the United States. Among the European countries doubts grew as to whether the United States would ever
really incur consequences of this dire order on their behalf.

Massive retaliation had so many practical defects that its credibility
was questionable. If it were not credible it could not be a deterrent,
since the value of a deterrent lies in threats which are so credible as never
to be tested. The alternative policy, slow to evolve, was one of flexible
response. This meant that the United States, in association with her Nato
allies, resolved that military incidents in Europe should be met at as low
a level of controlled violence as possible. Thus time would be bought in
an emergency during which the intentions of the opponent could be
examined and negotiations attempted. Nuclear weapons would not be
thrown wildly into the fray from the outset.

A vital complement of flexible response was a policy of graduated
nuclear deterrence. This policy requires that, once the existence of a
war rather than a minor international incident has been established, only

relatively small-scale tactical nuclear weapons should be used against an aggressor until such time as they prove to be inadequate. The policy of graduated nuclear deterrence seemed necessary for two basic reasons. First, it should replace the incredible, and therefore prospectively ineffective, policy of massive retaliation. The logic of this position is simple: small-scale nuclear weapons need not bring continental devastation, so it may be rational to use them; and if it is rational to use them, their use is genuinely to be feared; if the threatened use is genuinely feared the threat offered will not be tested, and deterrence succeeds because nuclear weapons are not used and the opponent does not advance. Secondly, small-scale nuclear weapons are required to back up a policy of flexible response, since flexible response is hardly flexible while conventional forces in retreat from other conventional forces have no recourse save to massive nuclear retaliation.

While small-scale nuclear weapons are necessary to substantiate policies of graduated nuclear deterrence and flexible response, large-scale intercontinental weapons remain in existence and may be seen to serve vital purposes. They remain in demand, first, to deter the possibility of a massive attack. An enemy might choose to ignore a limited war facility. Second, a massive capability is necessary to back up graduated deterrence and, thence, flexible response. If the use of small-scale nuclear weapons is to remain small-scale a constraint must be felt by the warring parties which is sufficiently strong to discourage them from expanding the areas and intensity of their hostilities. No more sobering constraint can be imagined than the damage which would result if small nuclear detonations were replaced by massive ones. In this way, then, defensive military capabilities in Western Europe can be imagined in the context of a closely interconnected hierarchical system, substantially controlled by the United States. Conventional forces substantiate a policy of flexible response; small-scale nuclear weapons substantiate a policy of graduated deterrence and back up flexible response; large-scale weapons substantiate massive retaliation, and back up graduated deterrence and flexible response.

Complications of no mean order are inherent in this sytem. Most prominent among these, at the theoretical level, is the difficulty of showing conclusively that the actual effect of the system would be to emphasise flexible response in the event of military incident. The ease with which the nuclear threshold can be crossed, the lack of any absolute distinctions among the range of nuclear weapons, the inclination of fighting armies to cap each other's destructive efforts; these and other factors combine to suggest that the whole structure might be totally unstable. In the nature of the case such a conclusion cannot be shown to be false. But the purpose of the system is to provide a stable deterrent; that is, one that is not challenged or used. It is supposed to provide defence and a kind of safety.

At the lower end of the hierarchy the prime requirement of stable defence is the maintenance of a substantial traditional force on which the flexibility of flexible response depends. If this force is inadequate it becomes merely a 'tripwire', capable of registering that an incident has occurred. But almost immediately the use of tactical nuclear weapons is then required. In this way the nuclear threshold is lowered and response has little flexibility. At the intermediate level, a convincing array of tactical nuclear weapons must be held in readiness in the general area of possible incidents. If this condition is not met three consequences must be faced. First, a 'tripwire' cannot work. Second, flexible response is not securely founded on a substantial local reserve of nuclear force which need not be used but which an enemy knows can be used. Third, graduated nuclear deterrence becomes an empty policy and, at the nuclear level, must be replaced by massive retaliation with all its dangers and disadvantages. At the topmost level, that of intercontinental nuclear capability, the capacity to mount a devastating riposte after an attack of any magnitude must be maintained. If it cannot be, an enemy may not be deterred from an attack at any level and the whole system is likely to collapse.

An essential fact about this system in relation to European defence is the dominant role played by the United States. The United States controls the overwhelming bulk of Western intercontinental nuclear weapons; ultimately her government controls most of the tactical nuclear weapons deployed in Europe; and she makes a substantial contribution to the troops deployed in conventional roles in Europe. What the government of the United States does with her military forces thus intimately affects the defence policies of the European governments. The most obvious pressure on the United States in this connection is that of economy. The most expensive item of her military capability as it affects Europe is men. If American troops in Europe are reduced and not replaced from other sources, then flexible response begins to look an empty policy and any forces remaining simply serve the 'tripwire' function. A way to avoid this outcome would be for the European governments to contribute more to the maintenance of the conventional response capability. But if American troops in Europe were reduced very radically indeed, graduated deterrence would be suspect regardless of the conventional efforts of the Europeans. The threat implied by the existence of nuclear weapons under American control carries conviction because of the presence of large numbers of American soldiers; if these were to become involved in a European battle the likelihood of nuclear weapons being used is high. But if very few American troops are present this likelihood may appear to be very much dimished. The threat offered by graduated deterrence thus becomes less credible and therefore less effective.

Developments at the topmost level of first-rank military strength are no less significant for Europe. A first-rank power has an obvious interest in maintaining a stable nuclear capability, that is, one which is unlikely to be used. Three sets of situations can disturb this stability: first, nuclear accident or misunderstanding of an opponent's intentions at times of crisis; second, the involvement of the first-rank powers in an outburst of violence initiated by a third party; third, technical developments which undermine the power of riposte. The two first-rank powers combine to reduce these dangers. They maintain close communications with each other. They attempt to 'institutionalise' crises. They show a good deal of caution in dangerous third areas, such as the Middle East. And they have combined in attempts to control nuclear weapons themselves. The first-rank powers have participated in general arrangements to limit the spread of nuclear weapons, first, by agreeing not to deploy such weapons in specific areas such as the Antarctic, the oceanbed, and in space; and second, by attempting to discourage other countries from developing possibly unstable nuclear capabilities. They have also entered into close bilateral negotiations directly affecting the deployment of their strategic weapons. Technical developments are a continuing source of anxiety to first-rankers: for example, if one first-rank power could develop an entirely effective antimissile defence system, deterrence would become unstable because the riposte capability of the other first-ranker would be thoroughly undermined and it would be open to attack. In advance of this situation, such a threatened power might feel obliged to attack first, while it still had the capability to do so. The two first-rankers have thus agreed to some mutual limitations in the deployment of their antimissile weapons. The two first-rankers have two further kinds of interests which draw them together. They both have numerous non-military claims on their resources and are thus both concerned with economy. They also have an interest in reducing mutual tensions in a general political sense, because their concern with military strength

B

would be thereby rendered less obsessive, economy could be more readily obtained, and the possibility of military incidents reduced.

THE DANGERS FOR WESTERN EUROPEAN DEFENCE

Continuing bilateral negotiations between the two first-rank powers present West Europeans with a number of defence problems. In an extreme and unlikely case, it is possible that the first-rank governments could achieve too close an accord for comfort. The combined first-rankers are a force of unassailable magnitude. If they agreed to a complete European settlement, the European governments might be unable to gainsay them, even though the settlement were highly uncongenial. More immediately, an agreement among first-rank powers which simply contributed to a radical reduction of American nuclear and conventional commitments in Europe would also create severe defence problems. First, there would be the problem of the possibility of Soviet bad faith; it is conceivable that the United States government might be, or might allow itself to be, duped. Second, there is the obvious geographical and political fact that the Soviet Union and the United States are not equally placed in Europe. Once removed, Soviet forces could be readily reintroduced, while reduction or removal on the American side is not so easily reversible. Whatever the condition of technology, the Atlantic is likely to remain a formidable barrier to the European deployment of American troops. More important, regardless of the excellence or otherwise of transportation facilities, it might be politically difficult for an American government to move back into Europe in times of trouble if this seemed to be a move back into unwelcome expense and risk. Much of past American foreign policy has been dedicated to keeping out of foreign, particularly European, quarrels, and this tradition is far from dead.

It is important in discussing contemporary Western European defence problems to remember that one is concerned with calculations about relative risks. If Western Europe were to find itself vulnerable, it does not follow that it would be brutally attacked. But it might very well follow that Western European governments would be unable to withstand more ordinary diplomatic pressures in negotiations affecting the welfare and safety of their countries. A government which has a substantial military advantage over another is the less likely of the two to compromise in a period of tension.

The European governments are thus linked intimately with the United States in their pursuit of safety by defence. This is a complicated relationship, which implants in Europeans a profound concern with the general pattern of American foreign policy and the movements of American opinion related to it. If the United States becomes involved in a severe conflict in a third area it seems likely that hostilities (certainly the effects of hostilities) could spread to Europe. Yet European governments are unlikely to exercise much influence over the full scope of American foreign policy while their military commitments in third areas are neglible. At the same time, unhappy entanglements, such as that with Vietnam, tend to produce a climate of opinion in the United States which stresses the desirability of a general reduction in the American military presence overseas, thus adversely affecting the policies of flexible response and nuclear deterrence in Western Europe. Similarly, the pressures which propel the United States into intimate negotiations with the Soviet Union might lead to a European settlement unacceptable to the European governments.

Western European governments are individually concerned with their safety; they are also concerned with one another's safety because of their geographic proximity and because of their close economic, cultural and political relations. But they have still wider concerns which intimately affect their strategic policies. They are confronted by an empire in Eastern Europe which is commonly found distasteful on two grounds: first, it contains large nuclear and conventional forces which raise the possibility, at least, of military pressure, if not attack from the East; second, the subjection of Eastern Europe is morally objectionable, in just the same way as subjection in Africa is objectionable to many African governments. Western Europeans thus have an interest both in the reduction of military forces in Eastern Europe, and in the cultivation of relations with the Soviet Union, and with the Eastern European governments themselves, whose consequences might be the relaxation of the bondage of fellow Europeans. These intentions are complementary in the sense that political policies in relation to Eastern Europe (the general recognition of the East German Democratic Republic, for example) may relax European tensions and provide a climate in which military reductions are possible. But there are two fundamental difficulties: first, negotiation about military forces in Europe means negotiation with the Soviet Union, and Western European governments, singly or collectively, cannot negotiate with the Soviet Union from a position of strength; second, the future subjection of Eastern Europe is primarily controlled by the ideology and interests of Soviet governments and these are difficult to calculate or to influence. To negotiate with the Soviet Union from strength the Western Europeans need the United States. Western European defence is thus haunted by a number of spectres: by Soviet bad faith, particularly important because it is likely to remain easier, in both psychological and logistic terms, for the Soviet Union to build up military strength in Eastern Europe than for the non-communist governments to do likewise in Western Europe; by the possibility of Soviet–American agreements and dispositions made in disregard of British and other European governments; by the possibility of a lessening United States commitment to Western Europe. In the contrary direction, the Western European governments are not likely to gain by an excessive emphasis on military strength in their territories, were this ever to prove politically possible for them, since overall tensions would be increased thereby and military stability consequently threatened. And such an emphasis, with such a consequence, would partially legitimate repressive Soviet policies in Eastern Europe.

THE FUTURE OF INTERNATIONAL SECURITY

Since its inception, the system of international strategic deterrence has seemed to provide Western Europe with a substantial measure of safety. Some of the main hazards of deterrence as a system of defence have been mentioned. The prospects of deterrence as the basis of a system of international security, currently dominated by the authorities of the Soviet Union and the United States jointly, are sometimes obscured by pressing national concerns for safety through defence. Gross instability in deterrence, and consequent loss of security for the world at large, is possible in three broad ways. There is the chance that one of the major powers might obtain a capability, or, equally dangerous, appear to obtain a capability, for launching an initial nuclear strike of such effectiveness as to disarm its opponent. This danger cannot ever be dismissed since no weapon yet produced, including the missile-launching submarine, has been beyond the capacity of human effort to destroy. There is, secondly, the long-appreciated danger of the dispersion of nuclear weapons among governments unable to control their deployment with restraint because of pressures of internal and external circumstances. There are, thirdly, the possibilities of accident, miscalculation, and of unauthorised use, all particularly acute during periods of high international tension and political confusion.

The powers attempt to meet these problems of instability in three broad ways. First, there are informal agreements and conventions. These can appear to relate to such substantial matters as informal understandings to restrict the size of defence budgets (which may reduce the chances of technical imbalance and dampen down the arms race generally). A clear difficulty with informal and tacit agreements as foundations of a system of international security is that there must be uncertainty about what exactly they are and what they amount to. In times of tension, when they would be most needed for the maintenance of international security, they would be most readily abandoned, thus adding to already heightened resentments and confusions. A reputed Soviet–American understanding to limit defence expenditures was quickly jettisoned as American embroilment in Vietnam became increasingly costly and more intensely identified with the interests of American governments. Some tacit agreements and understandings (and such have been a common feature of battle experience down the ages) may be a convenience for stable defence (one thinks, for example, of the advantages, in terms of cool strategic control, of the existence of tacit agreements relating to the patrol limits of military aircraft and nuclear submarines). But these are aspects of long-established techniques of military conflict and do not form the basis of a stable system of international security with the prospective capacity to resolve conflict.

Second, the search for stability can be directed to the negotiation of formal treaties. Numerous arms control treaties have been signed relating to limitations on atmospheric testing, limitations on the deployment of nuclear weapons in specific areas (Antarctica, the oceanbed, outer space), limitations on the export of nuclear weapons to nonnuclear countries and on their acquisition and development by nonnuclear countries, limitations on the deployment of antimissile systems by the first-rank powers, limitations on the number of land-based intercontinental missiles deployed by first-rankers. But treaties also have a number of disadvantages as the building blocks of an international security system. The major powers tend to agree to restrictions on themselves which are not in fact restrictions in any real sense. The partial Test-Ban Treaty, for example, is no limitation to a major power which already possesses tested weapons capable of explosions as great as could ever be necessary, even in a final holocaust, and whose underground testing facilities cover the development needs of smaller weapons. Similarly, there is no point in placing weapons in Antarctica, where they would be frozen; or on the seabed, where they could be observed and pillaged by an adversary's submarines; or on space platforms, which would be similarly available for close observation and interference by any power capable of space exploration. Treaties of any clear meaning are in their nature rigid constructions. They refer, inevitably, to the political and technological circumstances in which they are negotiated. In the nature of the case, an international security system in the nuclear age must be capable of rapid adaptation both to sudden political shifts in the international milieu and to unforeseeable technical developments. A series of fairly rigid treaties cannot supply the constant international monitoring of changing political and technical conditions which an acceptable security system would require. In addition, treaties create tensions and resentments both in themselves and in their negotiations: exclusive arms limitation negotiations between the United States and the Soviet Union create apprehensions about the possibilities of a first-rank world condominium; attempts to limit the spread of nuclear weapons can appear very one sided to a power such as France, which feels a strong motivation towards nuclear status. Another difficulty with treaties is that not all the relevant powers (France and China, for example) adhere to them in the first place. And powers which do adhere to them may cheat, or they can legally renounce their obligations. The Non-Proliferation Treaty has been signed by a number of powers, such as Japan, which are able to develop their own nuclear arsenals should they feel circumstances so require.

A third approach to stability manifests itself in the creation of international organisations. It has been in the pursuit of stable defence that organisations have made their greatest impact in Europe: Nato and the Warsaw Pact have for decades been the pillars of the Continent's defence arrangements. The UN was created to advance security on a universal scale but its impact on the daily conduct of international conflicts, in Europe and elsewhere, has been slight. Yet organisation for security has a number of advantages. First, it is flexible in the sense that, unlike a conference, an organisation is in a constant state of being and can take immediate notice of fresh international security problems as they arise. It does not have to be summoned laboriously into existence. Second, an organisation should not be the cause of resentments since its membership need not be exclusive. Similarly, it should provide an apparatus whereby otherwise disadvantaged smaller powers may exercise some influence on large powers. Third, it is a far less brittle creation than a treaty, which cannot survive the battering of states which interpret their treaty obligations differently. Fourth, an organisation, by its constant and active existence, has the opportunity to create a common language about the problems it is designed to tackle and to establish a staff of experienced international civil servants fully committed to the realisation of common international interests.

In the case of organisations for security at the universal level, the strain between general interests and local interests has been so great as to have a markedly debilitating effect. The UN can take notice of new international developments of almost any kind, and suffers from a lack of focus accordingly. The UN has come to include in its membership almost every state in the world, but the consequent diversity of interests pressed on the organisation is so great that united action is almost impossible. Similarly, small states can press their views upon major states in the UN, but they cannot commit major states to action, and by their persistence encourage major states to conduct their affairs outside the UN. Yet the UN has been a far from fragile organisation. There is every hope of its indefinite survival. The cost of this longevity has been a degree of flexibility and low achievement, which has pushed the UN towards the periphery of the practical conduct of international affairs. The range of problems which the UN may be called on to consider militates against the rapid evolution of common international values and effective instruments for their realisations in practice. It was the original intention of the Charter that the UN would have at its disposal substantial military forces organised by a Military Staff Committee responsible to the Security Council. But the powers were not prepared to assign military units to an international body which could not be relied on to use them in ways dictated by national defence requirements. A British army deployed by the UN in some remote conflict of no direct concern to Britain might have left Britain dangerously exposed in Europe. The tension between national and universal interests was too great for practical resolution.

It is possible that a kind of resolution of the demands of defence and security might prove practicable at a regional rather than a universal level. In Europe large military forces, equipped and supported by complete nuclear arsenals, confront each other in the fulfilment of defence policies which cannot guarantee safety. At the same time, the first-rank powers directly involved in this confrontation are jointly concerned to stabilise nuclear deterrence and economise on military budgets. The Western European governments have nothing to gain from high military tension in Europe, least of all from local nuclear war, but most of them are concerned for their own safety and for the maintenance of the American defence commitment in Europe. In consequence, Britain and West Germany are particularly concerned to maintain close communication on defence questions with the United States, both diplomatically and through the organisational structure of Nato. From this tangle of interests and commitments it might be possible to weave a European pattern of international security. A new European organisation, containing representatives of all the members of Nato and the Warsaw Pact, dedicated to the maintenance of European security, might prove congenial to all the powers currently seeking safety in Europe through policies of defence. A new security organisation could supervise any agreed arrangements on arms control in Europe. In the past, the first-rankers have always found difficulty in accepting the principle of international inspection of arms limitation agreements. Inspection by an international body in a limited part of Europe might prove far more congenial. Western European countries have a moral concern for involving the Eastern European countries in a European organisation and in opening them to some kind of international presence. If a new European security organisation could be developed to a point where national armies or parts of national armies, could be assigned to it, then the Soviet obsession with crude domination in Eastern Europe might be lessened. But any forces which could conceivably be assigned to an international security body would be more likely to take the initial form of contributions from relatively small European powers than from first-rank nuclear powers.

The relative decline of her own military strength, and the growing irrelevance of that strength to struggles in the non-European world, has led Britain to place Europe at the centre of her strategic calculations. But Britain does not merely have a defence interest in Europe. There is also an international security interest. Giving form to this international interest, without irresponsibly abandoning defence, is a central strategic task of the future. One of the themes of this chapter has been the stress on the discontinuity between the first- and second-rank countries and on the power of initiative which consequently lies in the hands of the first-rankers. But given that the first-rankers are not hostile to arms control and deterrence stabilisation, then European second-rankers like Britain do have a possible role in constructing the beginnings of effective international security. For these countries, this kind of role adds yet more qualifications to national sovereignty and national interest than those already created by their involvement in the network of international economic movements, institutions, and interests to which this essay turns next.

2 The economic habitat

It is not completely evasive to suggest that the international economy looks very important. Economic arguments, economic diplomacy, economic organisations often occupy the world stage to the virtual exclusion of more traditional dramatic forms.

The decline of old first-class military powers like Britain has contributed to this transformation. The old powers have no empires, they cannot go to war with the first-rank powers, nor can they go to war with one another, nor do they appear to have an interest in doing so. Their old strategic-diplomatic quarrels, formerly so absorbing and important, have faded as they have faded as military powers. The evolution of an apparently stable form of thermonuclear deterrence has had the effect of seeming to reduce the importance of the traditional international manœuvres and conjunctions whose consequence could formerly have been war. Large-scale war seems to have become an unusable arm of policy. In this way, the strategic-political world seems to require less attention than it once did. It can be powerfully argued that this is not actually so, but it is widely taken to be so. There has been a marked change in attitudes about the duties of government itself. Popular suffrage has caught up with statecraft. Governments are held widely responsible for providing conditions in which the prosperity and welfare of their citizens usually increase and never diminish. This duty has proved absorbing and difficult and is a highly sensitive feature of domestic politics, and therefore of international politics.

Though their interpretation may be no simple matter, some prominent characteristics of the international economy may be readily observed. One's eye falls first upon discontinuities. Most obviously there is a discontinuity between the communist and the non-communist systems. Neither of these systems is entirely coherent in itself but the gulf between them, so far at least, is fundamental. Trade across the gulf takes place on a large scale but there is no chance of Western governments or private interests participating in the substance or direction of communist economies. Similarly, though communist governments are active in some Western markets (the gold market is a notable example), there is no question of their acceptance of the value of international market forces nor of their unreserved participation in regulating them.

Within the non-communist world there are additional discontinuities. Marked among these is the discontinuity between the developing and the industrialised countries. Trade and investment crosses this gap, and many governments of underdeveloped countries are members of the international organisations, such as the International Monetary Fund, which attempt to regulate the non-communist international economy. These bridges do not generally confer much influence on the poorer countries. Differences in material conditions on each side of the divide are formidable and formidably resistant to amelioration. Nor is this discontinuity a clear one between two distinct worlds: in general terms, poor countries trade more heavily with rich countries than with one another. Individually their dependence on rich countries may therefore seem oppressive. Yet the Third World is, in economic terms, an extremely indistinct entity, and industrial countries, particularly those in Western Europe, together with Japan, experience an equally oppressive sense of dependence upon oil-producing states.

So the Western industrialised world, which has dominated the economic environment of Britain, is bordered by discontinuities, and, in general terms, these are conterminous with the defence system which is dominated formally or informally, by the massive nuclear umbrella of the United States. Within this economic fold there are minor discontinuities represented by tariffs and by non-tariff barriers to trade. There is also a more marked discontinuity, analogous to the thermonuclear discontinuity in the parallel defence system. In economic terms the United States also outranks her individual partners. Her wealth is greater that theirs. She is broadly less dependent on all forms of international trade than they are. She is relatively well endowed with raw materials, even oil. Her currency floods the international exchanges. The bulk of national monetary reserves are held in the form of dollars. The United States invests abroad on a greater scale than any other country, while the returns on her foreign investments, though large in absolute terms, constitute a very small proportion of her national income. The largest single group of multinational companies is American owned, and it effectively penetrates both the developed and the underdeveloped sectors of the non-communist economy.

Surveying the non-communist group of developed countries as a whole, one is aware of its very rapid, though unevenly distributed, rate of economic growth since the Second World War. The trading activities of these countries have similarly increased remarkably during the same period. The bulk of this increase has taken the form of trade in manufactured goods. It follows that the main increase in trade since 1945 has broadly taken the form of an increase in commerce among developed countries, not between these and the underdeveloped countries. Since 1965 the trade between developed countries has accounted for more than half of world trade. This feature has been matched by an increase in the movement of productive factors among Western developed countries, particularly of capital and enterprise. Large transnational companies provide an important medium within which these movements occur. There has also been an unexampled growth in the pool of liquid assets which can be moved swiftly from one currency to another. This phenomenon is not novel, but its scale is. A vast transnational market in currencies deposited outside their countries of origin has been created. The bulk of it takes the form of dealings in expatriate dollars, hence the market is commonly known as the eurodollar market. It operates primarily through the medium of private banks and banking consortia. The flexibility of this market makes it elusive to government control and sensitive to relatively small differences in national interest rates and to the anticipation of changes in currency exchange rates.

The increase in trade in manufactures between the Western industrial countries during the postwar period has been attended by a persistent inflation and by a growing sense that consumer-based prosperity may be based on ready supplies of cheap energy. The industrial countries have become competitors with one another and with the developing countries for the favours of oil-producers. The economic and political demands of the latter have revealed a measure of fragility in the economy of the West and have raised, in vivid form, political problems of Western solidarity and of the Western capacity to admit relative newcomers to their circle. Similarly, in no area has the massive international presence of transnational companies been more evident than in the supply of oil: they have negotiated with governments, they have been the medium through which the pressure of suppliers is exerted, and they have even seemed to operate a system of rationing among consumer nations.

A further, unexampled, development of the Western economic system has been the emergence of transnational intergovernmental organisations with the appearance, at least, of independent powers. The International Monetary Fund has begun to create international assets in the form of Special Drawing Rights (SDRs). These are claims not on individual governments but on the organisation and all its members. They are intended to be a final reserve asset, issued to governments, having a status analogous to that of gold. So far, SDRs comprise a small proportion of the total reserve assets available to governments. If they were to become a major element in the international monetary system then the IMF would be well on the way to becoming a kind of international central bank, creating credit, making it available to needy governments, and exercising an important role in the control of the world's money supply.

The other set of apparently powerful transnational institutions are those of the European Community. Though they have not gone far towards developing any of the characteristics of a central bank or finance ministry, a European Monetary Cooperation Fund has been established and the governments of the Community have committed themselves to the future creation of a common currency. Some of the members have already attempted to restrict the fluctuations in their mutual currency exchange rates. The Community tries to act as a whole in international tariff negotiations. Its governments are committed to a long programme of mutual harmonisation in fiscal, industrial, commercial and regional policies which, if successfully accomplished, must bring the Community to something like statehood.

CONFLICTS IN THE WESTERN ECONOMY

Many economists treat the non-communist international economy as a web of relations which creates a condition of interdependence among governments and economic institutions of all kinds. This is not an interpretation which necessarily conforms with political perceptions. It may be argued that the simple fact that national economies are connected to one another does not logically lead to the conclusion that governments are thereby somehow brought into a condition of close interdependence in which they should be able to treat mutual economic problems in a rational, cosmopolitan fashion. The dominating fact of the international economy may seem to be national power, and its irreducible basic component the national economy controlled by the sovereign state.

Western governments are held politically responsible for internal and external policies and for their effects. States are alike in this sense, but in terms of economic resources they are highly unequal. Units having the same political status but having very different degrees of economic strength cannot be interdependent, any more, so it might seem, than can states endowed with military resources of unequal size. Some may be relatively dependent, some relatively independent, while others may be in a position of relative dominance. Though they may interact they cannot be interdependent in any true sense.

This is a powerful perception, which many events seem to vindicate. A high level of international trade is not a novelty. Trade as a proportion of national products of advanced countries may even have declined a little during the course of the present century. At the beginning of the century Britain and Germany were particularly closely connected as economies, but the events of the First World War did not show the governments of these states to be aware of any close mutual interdependence. When one says that Britain is dependent on trade, one is not saying that British governments are in a condition of interdependence with the governments of her trading partners. It is simply the case that breaking these links would be more harmful to Britain than to countries less dependent on trade. A country whose trade and foreign investments contribute proportionately less to its national income is far more independent and powerful than Britain. The government of such a country may be able to exert pressure on the government of a country not so fortunate, since it will suffer proportionately less from economic disruption. Thus one might argue that the international economy is an arena dominated by national economic power, unequally distributed among states.

From this viewpoint the discontinuity between the United States and other individual countries in the Western international economy is a mark of the immense power of the United States. The other governments of the developed world are ranked in power below, often well below, the United States. A relatively strong government may be able to bring some influence to bear on the United States, but in no way does this signify the existence of an integrated system in which governments are interdependent. It has been estimated that the American economy accounts for over a third of the non-communist world's gross product. In general terms, countries such as Japan and Britain which trade with the United States are relatively dependent on American governments because, if trading links are cut, they are likely to suffer far more than the United States. A country which seizes American

investments in its territory harms the United States very little, while
retaliatory action by the United States (in the form of a trade embargo,
for example) is likely to be felt far more severely. Similarly, an inter-
ruption of supplies by oil-producing countries harms the United States
little, but causes extreme trepidation among other Western countries.
And those, such as Britian, which are vulnerable to this kind of pressure,
are not necessarily well placed to exercise any influence over United
States foreign policy.

The power conferred on American governments by the sheer size of
their domestic economy is complemented, it can be argued, by the fact
that the American currency is the basis of international monetary
arrangements. The bulk of currency reserves are held in the form of
dollars, and dollars are not convertible by the United States into gold.
They simply comprise a claim against the United States economy, and in
this domain the American government is sovereign. The American
government, in the last analysis, controls or fails to control the
American currency. Since the early 1950s the United States has run
intermittently massive deficits on its balance of payments. These have
been caused mainly by her large investments abroad, and by her expenditure on aid and, a larger element, on defence.

From the viewpoint of United States governments, the massive role
of the dollar among world currencies may represent the burdens and
responsibilities which the United States has shouldered as the leader of
an alliance of democracies. The deficits which have contributed to the
fulfilment of this role have provided the Western countries with a pool
of liquid assets which has eased the growth of world trade and contributed vastly to the remarkable economic growth of the economies
shattered by the Second World War. The ready supply of dollars
enabled other Western countries as a whole to maintain a seemingly
permanent balance of payments surplus, though this was not evenly
distributed among them. Direct overseas aid was a clear testimony to
American liberalism and responsibility. American overseas private investment, a sizeable contributor both to the deficit and to the creation
of the eurodollar market, performed the admirable function of spreading abroad American technical and managerial expertise, thus contributing an essential service to the efficiency and growth of other economies.
The eurodollar market itself contributed to the capital resources of
the Western economies and to their progressive growth and integration. Lastly, and in some eyes most importantly, American oversea
expenditure on defence reflected the most vital American role and her

determination to sustain it at costs to which other Western governments made totally inadequate direct contributions. The Western countries depended on the deterrent, both its nuclear and conventional components, which they did not pay for. And the American absorption in sublimited warfare in the Far East manifested the American refusal to adopt policies of appeasement similar to those which had so degraded the West as a whole before the Second World War.

Viewed from outside the United States, these arguments were not unflawed. The central role of the dollar was not created by the generosity of the United States but by the simple fact that the United States was overwhelmingly stronger than any other economy at the end of the Second World War. The dollar was strong and in short supply. As American deficits grew and dollars became plentiful the central role of the dollar remained. It seemed that the United States could pursue whatever policies she wished, in disregard of balance of payments problems. All she had to do was print more money which surplus countries had to acquire in large quantities simply in the process of maintaining official exchange rates under the system of fixed rates (fixed, that is, in terms of the dollar) created by the United States and Britain and institutionalised in the International Monetary Fund. The United States could ignore her own balance of payments.

In this way, it could be argued, American governments exported inflationary pressure by exporting large quantities of her currency. More important, particularly in French eyes, the system forced surplus countries, the non-American part of the system, to pay for the penetration into their own economies of American capital and large-scale American business enterprises, which further increased the power of the United States over them. Similarly, the surplus Western countries were forced into supporting American overseas military interventions, such as that in Vietnam, about which they often felt moral and political misgivings. Meanwhile, a country prone to deficits like Britain was placed directly in the power of the United States simply through dependence on dollar support for its currency. The system was created by the United States, it conferred great freedom and power on the United States, and the United States was in a position to force the burdens of any adjustments which became necessary on to the rest of the world. And when, in the early 1970s, the postwar system of fixed exchange rates was abandoned, largely as a result of American actions, the United States still dominated the international economy both by virtue of her size and the massive weight of dollars adrift in the system.

The view of the international economy as a power arena does not merely concentrate on the discontinuity between the United States and other countries, it emphasises the general point that states struggle with economic problems in the traditional style of power conflict. Thus both Britain and the United States have placed surcharges on imports in times of crisis in violation of international obligations. Efforts to maintain a system of public order in the international economy have not been notably successful. The IMF from its inception was intended to provide a regulated system of stable exchange rates which would bind all the member states and be conducive to orderly world trade. This general order was always fragile and collapsed in the early 1970s when countries revalued, devalued, and floated their currencies in ways which seemed best to suit their circumstances. Even the creation of SDRs by the IMF could be interpreted as an American device to take pressure off the dollar.

During the same period, the United States, through unilateral action, achieved one devaluation of the dollar substantially by forcing other countries to revalue their currencies upwards largely by threatening a trade war. Nor did EEC, before British entry, prove itself an entirely effective coordinator of monetary policies: most notably, Germany and France disagreed fundamentally on monetary policy, and acted out those disagreements on the international exchanges. And after her entry, Britain was hardly at the forefront of united action in dealing with cutbacks in Middle East oil supplies.

The fact that the United States has not been disposed to divest herself of sovereignty, it can be argued, both controls and reflects the nature of the Western economy. In the last analysis, states take their central decisions with their own interests primarily in mind. The most important decisions, in the nature of the arena, are taken by the government of the United States, and that government is moved primarily by internal political circumstances and bows minimally to the pressures of other governments whose economies confer a degree of strength on them. The imbalance of the Western defence system, which is shown in the overwhelming military power of the United States, may thus be argued to be replicated in the Western international economy.

INTERDEPENDENCE

The contrary view of the international economy does not ignore the existence of states, nor is it blind to the disorderly way in which the regulation of the international economy is attempted. What it emphasises is that this style is inappropriate to the economic facts of the setting. Interdependence is an economic reality which is not matched politically. Until this political realisation of economic facts takes place, governments will find themselves frustrated in the pursuit of individual economic policies simply because the authority of individual governments is not adequate to the tasks which they are set. The international economy of the West has outstripped the political resources available to run it. So the argument which stresses interdependence is not one which ignores the political habits of states, or the tendency of American governments to act out a kind of hegemony; it simply concentrates on the economic inadequacy of these political practices and tendencies.

The fact that discontinuities in trade and finance exist among Western industrialised countries does not necessarily create the conditions of national independence and power. Interdependence may in part be seen as the sensitivity of economic transactions between nations to economic developments within nations and within the group as a whole. Interdependence refers to mutual sensitivity, not to levels of economic transactions. From this viewpoint, the United States may be seen as highly interdependent with the other industrialised countries, even though her trade with them is not high measured in terms of the size of her own economy.

Given that interdependence refers primarily to sensitivity, a number of contemporary trends suggest that the realities of the international economy confound its image as an arena of autonomous national units. When demand in a national economy in the Western industrialised system increases, possibly as a result of government policy, imports into that economy tend to increase ahead of demand for domestic goods. This applies to the United States as well as to many other countries, particularly Britain. Additionally, the emphasis on manufactured goods in international trade, combined with the growing similarity both of Western tastes and Western costs of production, suggests that the sensitivity of demand to small changes in prices is likely to grow. At the same time, private companies, not only American companies, have developed a marked habit of seeking investment opportunities outside their national economies as zealously as they do inside them. They are certainly eager to exploit relatively small differences in national tax laws and social policies (in relation to regional development, for example). International investment, aided by the existence of the eurodollar market, has become more fluid and consequently more sensitive to differences in yields among national economies. In these and other ways, national markets are being drawn together into one large interconnected market based on the industrialised Western countries, whose tastes and political habits and problems show a measure of convergence.

The effect of this growing structural interdependence is that the autonomy of governments, not necessarily their sense of their own sovereignty, is undermined. Governmental economic policy depends for its effectiveness on the relative isolation of the national economy. If the national economy is merely a part of a larger structure the effects of policies are dissipated in this wider setting, or frustrated by larger trends emerging from it. These effects are becoming particularly pronounced in the context of increased demands on the economic performance of governments in all Western economies. The 'fine tuning' of an economy by a government is not possible, if it is possible at all in a free society, in the setting of a market which stretches beyond its national boundaries. For example, the growths of large international flows of capital tend to impose their own effects on national interest rates: raising a domestic rate to dampen a domestic economy may simply attract international funds (which in itself is likely to have a very undamping effect) while diverting internal demand for capital to the international market, a transition which is not easily prevented by governments.

Similarly, it may be argued that the growth of multinational businesses, particularly multinational banks and banking consortia, have undermined the effects of government policies relating to the direct regulation of industry and commerce. Tax obligations can be evaded by concerns whose activities are spread among a large number of units in a variety of countries, some of which may have deliberately lax standards in such matters. The same may be true of laws relating to monopolies and business practices generally.

If the effects of interdependence on internal economic policy merit wide comment, volumes have been written on its impact on national balance of payments policy. Here the approach which emphasises interdependence can curiously reverse interpretations from the viewpoint which stresses national powers and independence. The postwar international payments system was supposedly regulated by the rules of the IMF. In order to promote international stability this system required governments to maintain fixed exchange rates and to finance deficits in their balance of payments through the use of their own reserves and through IMF borrowings. Only when a 'fundamental disequilibrium' was shown to exist could a state alter the exchange rate of its currency. It can be argued that the breakdown of this system in the early 1970s was caused by the selfish scramble of national governments seeking their own advantage.

A somewhat different view stresses the fact that the IMF system, in its most fundamental nature, was based on national autonomy and the fragmentation of the international economy in national units. Though disturbing international capital movements could occur, the system assumed (and, in a sense, required) that effective national barriers to financial transfers could be imposed. Since the creation of the IMF the international movement of capital has become progressively easier, national governmental control over it more difficult, and the disruption which might result were such control possible and imminent so great as to injure rather than to benefit the country following such a course. It is arguable that the consequent change in the level of interdependence has been so great as to constitute a change in the nature of the international economy which outdates the assumptions behind the establishment of the IMF. The run on sterling in 1947, which had profound effects on British foreign policy, amounted to a maximum daily speculation of about 100 million dollars. In May 1971 over 1,000 million dollars moved into Germany in forty minutes to take advantage of a possible upward revaluation of the mark. In these kinds of circumstances, one could argue, the conditions which made the IMF arrangements possible have changed. Governments resort to individual defensive policies, floating their currencies most notably, because the political strength of international organisations is not consonant with the nature of the international economy, and governments are left with only inadequate traditional alternatives. They respond to the loss of their autonomy by the use of their inadequate sovereignty.

Stress on interdependence does not distinguish the present from the past in simple terms of the increase or otherwise in the total value of trade. What is being stressed is the increased sensitivity of economic transactions to one another in the international economy as a whole. This sensitivity places limitations on what governments can achieve. More important, from this viewpoint, it places on them a responsibility to consider the whole economic setting in making their economic dispositions.

EUROPEANS AND THE INTERNATIONAL ECONOMY

The pattern of the strategic setting is, in a sense, repeated in the economic setting. Even the viewpoint which stresses interdependence acknowledges the existence of distinct asymmetries in the international economy. The size and strength of the internal market of the United States does mean that if the American government imposes barriers to trade other countries are likely to be more affected than the United States. The international dominance of the dollar means that the United States has a degree of monetary autonomy lacking in many other countries. If the United States has an 'easy money' policy it is difficult for other countries to maintain policies of 'tight money' because of the massive inflow of funds this is likely to cause. The reverse does not fully apply because the size of the American economy means that inflows into the United States erode but do not necessarily undermine 'tight money' there. Similarly, the scale of American investment overseas and the overall size of American multinational companies means that American company law and taxation policy have greater impact overseas than do reverse policies. American military dominance may thus be seen to be mirrored in the international economy, and simple consultations and conjunctions among the second-class governments do not alter this basic position.

Also reflecting the international strategic setting, economic vestiges of Britain's former imperial role persisted after the decline of Britain from the first rank of states. Sterling continued to be very much used in trading transactions, and to be held as a currency reserve in other countries long after the Second World War. Indeed, British deficits during and after the war provided a useful service to the international economy through the provision of needed international liquidity, though in this function the United States soon replaced Britain. But because the British economy was a small one, in which imports accounted for a high level of internal expenditure, sterling was a weak currency which, contrary to some foreign thinking, conferred few benefits, and little autonomy, on British governments. A high dependence on imports, coupled with an imperial propensity to export capital, commonly placed Britain's balance of payments in a parlous condition. And British governments could not ignore the balance of payments in the style of American governments because of the relative weakness of the British economy and the availability of other assets into which holders of sterling could transfer. The effects on Britain in terms of forced retreats from fixed exchange rates, inflationary pressure, low economic growth and general havoc wrought with domestic economic policies, are too familiar to require emphasis.

However, the special situation of the British currency has changed to a degree in recent years and Britain has moved more into line with other second-class countries. The relative importance of sterling balances has declined as other balances, particularly dollars, have increased. The countries of the old sterling area have diversified their trade and have consequently built up other reserves. The currencies of other former first-rank powers, such as Japan and Germany, have become attractive as international assets. Other countries, particularly European countries, have in the past shown marked readiness to support sterling with short-term credits. The British government has ceased to regard the sterling area as an extension of the British economy. Official efforts to restrain the export of capital from Britain have come to apply to the old sterling area countries just as to other countries. And, perhaps most important, though the impact of speculation on sterling has not lessened, sterling has ceased to be unique in this respect. In recent years, for example, speculative movements out of francs and into marks have equalled, and probably exceeded, speculative movements affecting sterling.

As Britain moved towards the status of an ordinary European power in strategic terms so she has done so in economic terms. Just as Britain retains some overseas strategic liabilities, so she retains economic liabilities arising from foreign holdings of sterling and its use in speculative and other transactions. British liabilities are British liabilities, and they are somewhat greater than those of other second-class powers. But overall trends, coupled with the physical smallness of Britain have conspired to put British governments into a class of governments, and among these they are not unique, though the British economy, through its high propensity to import goods and services and to export capital, is likely to confer even less economic autonomy on British governments than some other second-class governments are likely to enjoy.

Britain is now a part of what is at least a customs union in Western Europe and what is planned to become very much more. British governments are locked with other Community governments in the obligation to seek common policies both within the Community itself and towards the external world. The connectedness of the international economy means that these two sets of problems cannot be placed into separate compartments. Whether the Community governments should respond more to the Western international economy seen as an arena of conflict between states or to the same economy seen as a system of interdependent economic impulses and policies, will be examined later in this essay. As a problem for Europeans this probably outranks all others.

Associated with it is the question of the attitude they should take towards the apparent dominance of the United States in the international economic system. The link here with the principal problems of defence is a close one. To point to these basic problems of attitude is to raise a further problem of fundamental substance: whether the European will be able to arrive at common attitudes at all.

Although these fundamental problems underlie most others, the actual difficulties which the European governments face are practical in form. Having largely acquired a common external tariff the Community governments must decide what to do with it, how to use it in their external trade policies. Having resolved to create a common currency they must face the formidable practical problems of achieving this end. Being plagued by the same energy crisis they must decide whether they can agree common policies for dealing with it.

At the same time they must face the monetary problems of the international economy as they present themselves as a whole. Among these is the set of problems familiarly grouped together as the 'liquidity problem'. At present a wide variety of currencies are used as reserve assets—dollars, pounds, francs, marks and yen, to which must now be added SDRs. Lurking not far in the background is a more traditional material, gold. The liquidity problem traditionally refers to the problem of financing world trade. As trade grows, more money is required to finance it. From the 1950s the dollar provided the necessary liquidity so effectively that a large number of countries have substantial dollar holdings which take the appearance, at least, of final reserve assets, being no longer even theoretically convertible into the traditional final reserve asset, gold, by the United States government. So in a way the world, for the present, has plenty of liquidity. But the liquidity problem remains in a number of senses. Some governments have been reluctant to accept settlements in dollars simply because there are so many of them. Though there are plenty of reserves, the question of reserve assets thus remains open. Some governments, particularly French governments, have favoured the reconstitution of 'real' assets, principally in the form of gold. Other governments are not anxious to accept the erratic disciplines of a commodity so scarce and so liable to the fortuitous fluctuations of both the mining industry and of the policies of the two principal producers, South Africa and the Soviet Union. The further development of SDRs appeals to rationalists in monetary affairs. Seeing that monetary affairs themselves are rarely entirely rational, some combination of SDRs and gold might prove acceptable.

The sheer size of liquid assets in the system creates a massive liquidity problem. In one week in February 1973 the West German Bundesbank, while operating a range of direct controls, still had to acquire about 6,000 million dollars in a vain effort to hold down the exchange rate of the mark. These dollars constituted only a small part of the total available on the eurodollar market.

In a sense, then, the greater world liquidity, the greater is the liquidity problem. The resort of allowing currencies to fluctuate absolutely freely is complicated by the plentiful availability of forms of liquidity which do not enjoy wide confidence: rapid movements of money, in its various plentiful forms, could play havoc with completely free exchange rates and bring international trade to a virtual standstill. The general abandonment of fixed rates early in 1973 did not mean that governments ceased to intervene to try to regulate currency movements.

Freely moving exchange rates raise not only the general problem of speculative instability, they also raise a special problem for the European Community. The Community governments cannot commit themselves completely to the free movement of their mutual exchange rates if they are to harmonise their economic policies and create some kind of common currency. Yet agreeing to fixed European currency exchange rates requires a high degree of Community support for the weaker currencies, like sterling, and this is not to be assumed as an indefinite commitment. The joint European float of early 1973 did not include sterling, partly for this reason, though it did include the currencies of some non-EEC countries. From the viewpoint of national sovereignty, freely moving exchange rates may appear to confer independence on governments in their pursuit of domestic goals: but movements of funds (in Britain's case particularly) may depress a currency's exchange rate to such an extent as to create an inflationary rise in the prices of imports and force from a government so threatened a number of actions contradicting the principles of both floating exchange rates and autonomy in internal policies. From the viewpoint of interdependence, the existence of a large international money market requires an international policy to regulate it. It can further be argued that the Community is too small to tackle overall world currency problems in a rational manner.

A second set of traditional problems remains to be mentioned, and these are closely linked with misgivings about the role of the United States in the present setting, and the possible future role of the IMF. These are the problems of adjustment among the national economies in the international system. In broad terms, all the countries in the system are in a perpetual condition of imbalance in their international payments. Surpluses in some countries are generally the complement of deficits in other countries. The recent deficits of the United States have thus been the complement of the surpluses of the rest of the world. The regulation of exchange rates to iron out these imbalances creates political problems of adjustment. A country whose currency falls in value relatively to other currencies suffers increases in the prices of its purchases abroad and thus imports inflationary pressure, as British governments have found. A country whose currency rises in value cures a payments surplus by reducing the competitiveness and profitability of its exporting industries, and opens its markets to cheap imports, thus reducing the general profitability of home industries, and perhaps creating home unemployment.

Because the regulation of exchange rates is related to hard underlying political effects such as these, 'ordered' adjustment in the recent past has been partly a process of tough international negotiation between governments. Deficit countries of relatively minor strength like Britain have had to devalue in reluctant obedience to balance of payments discipline. But surplus countries under the postwar system of fixed rates were not seen to be under the same pressure to revalue upwards. A regulated exchange system may thus seem to accentuate differences in national economic power. A freely floating system may expose all, deficit countries and surplus countries, to the effects of speculative movements which create the movements in rates which they anticipate. Again, the logic of interdependence may seem to require an authoritative international organisation able to determine the general pattern of exchange values, allocate the burdens of adjustment equitably between deficit and surplus countries, and generally to manage the international monetary system though the control of the creation and allocation of final reserve assets. No such organisation exists, though the IMF has some of the required formal characteristics. The political strength of an organisation capable of transnational functions of such an order must be formidable. Yet the opposite sort of expedient, whereby most countries float nervously to the accompaniment of miscellaneous government interventions, may prove extremely unstable and far more harmful to the growth of world trade than the old IMF system of imperfectly maintained fixed rates.

NATIONAL AND INTERNATIONAL INTERESTS

Beneath all the technicalities of international trade and finance lie the political interests of governments and their constituents. But these interests are not wholly national in character. The Western economic system as a whole is a resource of its members. Its collapse would affect all the national economies, catastrophically in many cases.

The old IMF system of fixed exchange rates was abandoned largely because it proved a burden to its most powerful member, the United States. Because the dollar was the *numeraire*, the standard, of the international monetary system the United States could not devalue her own currency, since all other currencies, whose values were signified in terms of dollars, moved as the dollar moved. They were marks on the dollar ruler, and if the ruler moved they all moved with it. This came to be felt as an intolerable limitation on the sovereignty of the United States as her balance of trade slipped into deficit. The IMF, under the old system, could not force countries in surplus on their balance of payments to revalue upwards. The limitation on the power of the United States to devalue unilaterally was thus compounded by the lack of power in the international organisation to achieve the same result by requiring other countries to revalue. So the system broke up as the United States used her relative immunity to the harsh effects of trade dislocation to pressure surplus countries, particularly Japan, into currency revaluations. As more and more countries, including Britain, allowed their currencies to float the role of the *numeraire*, essential to a fixed-rate system, became redundant.

Given that an orderly system of trade and payments is an international interest, it would seem to follow that the principal trading countries of the West are faced with two basic problems. First, without re-establishing fixed rates there should nevertheless be bands of exchange rate variations capable of giving stability without rigidity. If this is so, then some kind of *numeraire* other than the dollar must be established. Even if the United States moves into balance of payments surplus and the dollar once again becomes a strong currency, a not unlikely prospective consequence of rising international energy costs, American governments are still unlikely to relish the resumption of the postwar role of the dollar as an undervalued *numeraire*. Second, given that all countries, not least Britain, are reluctant to change their domestic economic policies in response to the demands of their balance of payments positions or in response to international agreements to maintain specific currency parities, practical international arrangements must not be too ambitious in their demands on national governments. But if no effective demands are made on governments, particularly in relation to the allocation of burdens of adjustment between deficit and surplus countries, then the system as a whole will be subject to sudden shocks, persistent resentments, and, more important, to a growth of regional solutions within the Western industrialised circle.

It can be powerfully argued that international trade and investment move in accordance with the existence of an underlying political system. The growth of international trade and investment among industrialised countries since 1945 has substantially conformed to the boundaries of the international political system centred on the United States. The United States provided the overall defence of the system and the United States took the lead (assisted by Britain) in integrating the ex-enemy states into the Western economy and its institutions. Similarly, the United States exercised a degree of leadership in reducing tariff barriers under the auspices of the GATT; the dollar provided the basic liquidity for the postwar growth in Western trade; American-based transnational companies exported American technical and managerial skills; the United States (assisted by Britain) established and maintained the fixed rate monetary system of the IMF which permitted Japan and West Germany to maintain low exchange rates and longstanding surpluses on their balance of payments. So the core of the postwar international economic system, for all its proliferation of international organisations, was the leadership of its most powerful individual member. And the essence of the leadership of the United States lay in her perception of her role as being that of guardian of free men from the encroaching might of the Soviet Union, and, a little later, of China. Over recent years a number of fundamental changes have taken place in this economic-political international system. The most important of these has been the slackening of the Cold War and the growing diplomatic association between the United States and the Soviet Union. This has powerful implications for the Western defence system, as we have seen. It also has powerful implications for the Western economic system. If, for example, the United States ceases to believe that her values are under fundamental threat in the Far East, then Japanese association with American defence ceases to be a vital American interest: American governments can therefore use their economic strength more vigorously than they already have to pressure Japanese governments without fundamental anxiety about the defence consequences of possible Japanese resentments. Similar considerations apply to Europe.

The postwar political-economic system of the West was founded on the enlightened leadership and strength of the United States. It has been suggested above that the United States still remains at the centre of the system, but she has become something less than indulgent. And the peripheral parts (Japan and Western Europe) are now a good deal stronger despite their collective dependence on external supplies of oil. This would seem to indicate that the system is likely to move in one of two possible directions: either in the direction of an economic-political system with control less centralised in the United States, in which case the role of transnational organisations such as the IMF must be strengthened; or in the direction of schism and, as a consequence, the pursuit of greater regional autonomy at the periphery, in which case the tendency of the United States to reduce the level of her commitments to the network of Western defence could be accelerated. It will be argued in a subsequent chapter that Britain is likely to remain interested in the continuation of the American defence involvement in Europe: the logical extension of this for Britain is a stress on interdependence within the Western economy as a whole.

3 The institutional habitat

The traditional institutions of a world society weak in its sense of community were the sovereign state, diplomacy and war. The sovereign state provided its citizens with political order and physical safety. The society of states provided the world at large with a political structure accurately reflecting and preserving its immense variety yet simple in its sovereign units. Diplomacy was the means whereby these units of world society expressed their interests and conducted their relations. Diplomacy was also a world institution in the sense that it ameliorated the rigidities and conflicts of a society made up of identical units, sovereign states, of unequal strength and differing values. The existence of a threat of war was an essential support of the institution of diplomacy. Without it, the reality of the changing distribution of power among sovereign states could not be accommodated. States changed, not in their nature, but in their capabilities and in their immediate demands on one another. Diplomacy could not confer flexibility on international society without the legitimate threat of war because, in the last analysis, power based on war potential was the only means of adapting the notion of sovereignty to the changing reality of the distribution of human and material resources among states. Without this most real aspect of state power, diplomacy would have been reduced to subtle but trivial conversations among cultivated men. The threat of war, however distant, was an essential contribution to the seriousness of diplomacy and to the adaptability of world society. War was a form of mutual adjustment whereby some states were forced to accept rather more change than would otherwise have been congenial to them. War did not change the essential nature of international society. The conclusion of a war meant the renewal of diplomacy in conditions more closely adapted to the realities of the uneven distribution of power among otherwise equal states.

Each of these three institutions has been qualified and changed in modern times. Political movements and ideas, relating typically to the pursuit of equality and social justice, have tended to reduce the state from its status as the absolute form of internal social order to the status of an instrument whereby the social goals of political movements may be attained. The state becomes secondary to underlying social and political realities. Yet states have not thereby been rendered harmless international entities. In the twentieth century sovereignty has been seized by manic groups proclaiming goals of world domination. The existence of the modern state has not been conducive to the existence of civilised order at the national or international levels. So, perhaps unfairly, the state itself has become suspect as a form of social order, particularly in Europe. Just as the state's capacity to provide order has been questioned so has its capacity to provide safety. In the age of nuclear weapons the state cannot defend its citizens from the threat of annihilation which is at the core of nuclear deterrence; nor is it desirable that it should attempt to do so if the stability of deterrence is to be maintained. The autonomy of the modern industrialised state has also been undermined by transnational forms of economic activity. The Western state is so penetrated by impulses and organisations common to the community of industrialised states that it no longer constitutes, in itself, a mechanism adequate to the solution of many of the problems which assail its citizens. Though economic penetration is not new, its political impact has become greater as the role of the state in the economy has increased in response to political demands, and as the state's capacity to meet the requirements of this increased role has proved defective. In a sense the state no longer creates order, but is dependent on the maintenance of order at the international level. This is clearly the case in relation to the deployment of nuclear weapons in an international system of deterrence, but it is no less so in relation to the transnational economy. A Western state which attempts to stop domestic inflation in conditions of sustained international inflation is unlikely to be wholly successful.

Diplomacy has shared the impact of changing ideas and new realities in international society. A network of transnational relations has developed in the circle of the Western industrialised nations to which the world of traditional diplomacy can contribute little. The traditional diplomatist is not skilled in the arcane detail of the international problems raised by transnational monetary relations. The relationship of diplomacy to the exertion of power based on the war potential of states has altered too. War in the earlier part of the twentieth century

involved so many people so outrageously that the notion developed
that it was the duty of diplomacy to establish and operate international
organisations, notably the League of Nations, which would have the
effect of reducing and eventually abolishing the role of war in the
relations between states. Diplomacy was expected to break the link
between itself and war. This massive reform proved abortive because
of the uncertain authority of security institutions at the global level.
Diplomacy has remained absorbed in the possibility of war and in
preparing for it. Yet in the nuclear age this traditional concern has
produced untraditional consequences. Defence alliances have become
far more than temporary conjunctions among impermeable states.
Nato is a structure which exercises a measure of transnational control
over national military forces and which attempts to present a threat of
permanent readiness for war in Europe. The growth of transnational
intergovernmental organisations has been particularly marked in the
international economy. Additionally, the relations between governments in the Western circle have multiplied to a point at which almost
all the departments of state administration conduct relations across
national boundaries. Diplomacy has lost its exclusive place in the
contacts between governments. The attempt to create large-scale
conditions of growth, and to raise the international standing of British
governments, has led Britain to enter a transnational organisation, the
European Community, which evades exact categorisation but which
certainly exists beyond the parameters of traditional diplomacy in its
concern for transnational social and economic harmonisation and in its
direct legislative impact upon the citizens of different states.

The traditional institution of international war has undergone perhaps the most marked change of all. The clear capacity of nuclear
weapons to destroy the fabric of national and international society has
rendered problematic the status of war as the instrument of the state.
An instrument whose use is likely to destroy its user exercises a kind of
power in its own right, and it has become a concern of states to make
mutual arrangements to control this power. In a sense, nuclear weapons
constitute a common enemy which states attempt to incarcerate by
their joint policies. Nuclear weapons have also widened the discontinuity between the first-class powers and lesser powers upon which
this essay has already dwelt. The creation of a group of second-class
governments, to which British governments belong, has undermined
the myth of statehood in Western Europe and has rendered possible
an approach to the functions of government which does not start from

the structural premises of inviolable sovereignty. Yet the practical and psychological changes wrought by modern weapons on the nature of statecraft may in the long term prove less significant than the growth of systems of international and transnational relations in which the threat of war plays no part. Governments negotiating on their monetary relations and arrangements do not as a rule bring to play their war capabilities. Negotiations such as these are not a twentieth-century novelty, but the very sharp rise in their political importance since the Second World War challenges traditional high statecraft as the fundamental core of international relations. Large systems of international and transnational relations exist to which war is an irrelevance.

WORLD SOCIETY AND SYSTEMIC CONTROL

At the centre of the traditional view of the international institutional habitat lies the sovereign state. All other institutions grow out of this institution. The state-centric view is one which can accept change wrought by the shifting capabilities of states, but it cannot encompass the structural transformation of states because of the changeless quality of sovereignty. The static image of international institutions which the state-centric view engenders has often created doubts as to its moral, intellectual and practical validity. An attempt to evolve a view which is more dynamic takes as its starting point not the longstanding existence of states but the existence of a world society in which human relations are not walled in by the state and in which problems occur to which the strict application of state sovereignty can offer no effective solution. This view recognises the existence of important elements in world society which are not states and it accepts the necessity of international institutions, both now and in the future, which are not built from irreducible and impermeable blocks of state sovereignty.

In part, this view is founded on observation and experience. International relations are not exclusively relations between states. Transnational relations, networks of relations among groups which are not themselves states and which operate across state boundaries, comprise much of the fabric of world society. Religion, trade, capital, fashion, science, are all terms which denote forms of transnational behaviour which are not dominated by the notion of state sovereignty. Multiple loyalties and transnational forms of personal life are a concrete reality. A British subject who is also a Roman Catholic, a scientist of international repute and a loyal executive of a multinational pharmaceutical company may go through life without any sense of political or social abnormality. Personal transnationalism is as real as the networks of relations between transnational organisations. Transnational churches may participate in an equally transnational ecumenical movement. A multinational company competes and makes agreements with other multinational companies, raises funds in a variety of currencies, accepts capital assistance from governments and negotiates with governments. Trade unions may form international coalitions to bargain with multinational companies. Transnational companies, airlines for example, may form alliances to press their interests on governments. A British nationalised industry or a local authority may raise capital on the eurodollar market.

The existence of transnational 'layers' of international society is not in doubt. More significant in the present context are the relations of governments to transnationalism. At a given moment a British government may be absorbed in problems of labour relations at the British plant of a multinational company, with a speculative movement out of sterling, with negotiating a change in the European Community's common agricultural policy, with a legal action relating to the apparent monopoly practices of a foreign-owned company in Britain, with securing orders for an aircraft produced by a consortium of British and European companies, with urging the case for a more effective role for the IMF, with negotiations on tariffs in the context of both the EEC and the GATT, with the impact on the British contribution to Nato of prospective American troop reductions, with a transnational air incident perpetrated by a terrorist group. In issues like these a British government deals with foreign groups and private organisations which operate within British society, with transnational markets in goods and capital, with an intergovernmental organisation having a direct regulatory authority within Britain, with relations between intergovernmental organisations, and with an intergovernmental organisation under whose aegis the bulk of British military forces are deployed. In an international society conceived as sets of transnational relations the strict notion of sovereignty is an irrelevance, since the problems to which governments address themselves do not arise and cannot be resolved strictly within the setting of one state's boundaries. When issues of domestic policy cannot be disentangled from a web of transnational issues the notion of foreign policy as a set of distinctive contacts between sovereign states collapses, and is replaced by a generalised search for appropriate modes of authoritative response by governments to problems which relate not to the collisions

of state sovereignties but to the problems of a society whose regulation
is impeded by state sovereignty.

The impact of transnationalism on British governments takes three
practical forms. First, the search for the benefits of scale to the British
economy has contributed to entry to the European Community. The
Community is concerned with both scale and the regulation of scale.
It attempts to create a regulated transnational market in goods, capital,
enterprise and labour. The transnational harmonisation of government
policies in these areas is necessary both to achieve scale and to provide
the essential conditions for the regulation of scale on the part of the
Community itself. The Community therefore widens the range of
transnational impulses at play on British society and attempts to create
an effective form of legitimate transnational government appropriate
to the scale of those impulses. Second, Britain is affected by transnational organisations and markets which neither the Community
nor a British government has the jurisdiction to regulate effectively.
There therefore exists a motivation, of uncertain political strength, to
increase the competence of intergovernmental transnational organisations, or to create new ones, with a comparable range of operations.
Thus a renewed IMF might be able to make an impact on the problem
of the 'slop' of dollars among other currencies. Similarly, the investigation, and eventually the regulation, of the operations of multinational
companies might be entrusted to a new arm of the GATT. Third, the
pursuit of goals formerly assigned to the domain of high sovereign
statecraft leads British governments into a profound involvement with
intergovernmental organisations having a direct impact on what were
once the instruments of the sovereign. Defence in the nuclear age has
compelled British dependence on a transnational military structure
concerned with deterring military incursions into Western Europe.
To the degree to which British governments commit themselves to the
achievement of security in Europe they must also commit themselves
to the construction of even wider transnational organisations with a
degree of regulatory authority over national military forces.

The view which fixes primarily on the existence of transnational
systems of relations within world society has little place for the concept
of foreign policy as the external actions of the sovereign state. World
society creates transnational world problems and the nature of foreign
policy is transformed thereby. A government confronted by such
problems is misguided if it concentrates on applying to them the
sovereignty of the state, which is inadequate to their solution. Trans-

c

national problems require the attentions of effective transnational governmental institutions. The aim is to control systems of relations which affect citizens but which individual governments cannot regulate effectively. Thus diplomacy is replaced by the intergovernmental search for forms of organisation and authority appropriate to systems of international and transnational relations which demote states as providers of order and safety and which blunt their instrumental capabilities to control the economic, military, and social forces which affect the lives of their citizens. Systemic control is the goal of intergovernmental relations and its institutional realisation bears little relation to the maintenance of the place of sovereignty and traditional diplomacy in world society.

BETWEEN TWO WORLDS

The world of transnational control does not obliterate the traditional world of states, diplomacy and power. The two worlds exist together. The institutions of world society therefore present a prospect of extreme complexity, to which a single line of analysis is inapplicable because of the different kinds of conceptual parameters which may be validly brought to bear. However, some of the problems created by the existence and intermingling of the two worlds may be simply tabulated.

1. Transnational economic relations cannot grow in the absence of any kind of underlying political order. The prosperity of Britain in the nineteenth century was created by the network of trade and capital movements whose foundation was an international order in which Britain played the major role. In the earlier part of the twentieth century this international order collapsed and the associated economic system was shaken to the detriment of the prosperity of Britain. After the Second World War the regeneration of the international economy was founded on a new international political order in which Britain came to play a far from powerful part. The new order's centre lay unmistakably in the United States and depended on the strength of the United States for its stability. The postwar growth of transnational activity and transnational organisations were thus linked closely with the United States in three ways: first, the strength of the American national economy lay at the core of the rapid expansion of American-based multinational companies and of the international monetary dominance of the dollar; second, the defence of the international association within which transnationalism developed most strongly depended on

the military power of the United States; third, the United States chose
to operate a foreign policy which stressed the role of intergovernmental
transnational organisations. The United States played a leading part
in creating and operating the IMF, the GATT, Nato and many others.
These close links between transnationalism and American foreign
policy mean that if American governments, concerned with American
interests, shift the direction of American foreign policy, transnationalism in all its manifestations could be undermined. When the United
States felt herself to be the champion of the free world, transnationalism, governmental and otherwise, was a means whereby American
influence expressed itself. During this period intergovernmental organisations generally relied heavily on the United States while conferring
many benefits on Western and associated countries at large. Many
currencies, notably those of Japan and West Germany, were allowed
under the old IMF arrangements to be maintained at low dollar
exchange rates. Nato relied on American nuclear and non-nuclear contributions. Similarly, the United States smiled on the early development
of the European Community as a new pillar of Western strength, even
though some features of EEC policies struck at her economic interests.

The period of harmony between transnationalism and American
foreign policy seemed to begin to wane as the United States grew
weary and sceptical of her chosen role as the Western colossus, as other
Western countries began to enjoy a standard of wealth not greatly
inferior to her own, as the international strength of the dollar gradually turned to weakness, and as relations between the United States and
the Soviet Union became closer and even themselves began to develop
a transnational quality in their attention to the control of first-rank
arsenals. The existence of the dollar exchange standard did not prevent dollar devaluations as the United States brought direct pressures
to bear on surplus countries to secure revaluations. The maintenance
of American troop levels in Europe seemed to become conditional
on West Germany, and perhaps other countries, mopping up surplus dollars as required. Regardless of bargains of this kind, political
pressures in the United States Congress for general reductions of overseas American military establishments grew. At the same time the
members of the European Community were urged to change their
common agricultural policy and it seemed possible that the Community would become an economic enemy of the United States.

The association of transnationalism and American foreign policy
creates two kinds of difficulties. First, transnationalism can be interpreted

as American imperialism and transnational intergovernmental organisations as means of propagating American values and interests. Second, movements in the transnational stratum which are not congenial to United States governments may be interpreted by them as direct assaults on American interests. The prospect of withdrawal of United States support for transnational organisations such as the IMF, Nato, and the EEC might cause British governments either to hasten to the side of the United States, placing absolute priority on the traditional unwritten Anglo-American alliance in which Britain would be so minor a partner as to rank as a vassal, or to stress the increased integration of Western Europe towards the goal of a new first-rank statehood. Neither prospect is likely to be attractive to Britain. While the links between transnationalism and American foreign policy persist then intergovernmental organisation must be particularly sensitive to United States foreign policy. The transnational stratum is deeply penetrated by the power and interests of a first-rank state.

2. By definition, intergovernmental transnational organisations can only be established by governments. In embarking on such enterprises governments may be moved far more by traditional diplomatic interests than by notions of systemic control. The British entry to the Community can be interpreted simply as a means of obtaining greater foreign policy leverage on the other Community governments and of increasing Britain's status in the world at large through her possible accession to economic strength and through her diplomatic influence on the Community as a whole. Efforts to extend the role of the IMF can be seen as schemes to reduce American power and increase outside influence on the disposition of what remains of it. Nato, in this light, is a means whereby the lesser European states obtain cheap defence and, doubtfully, a degree of influence on American strategic policy-making. The GATT can be taken to be an instrument with which American governments can attack the more distasteful trading policies of the European Community.

The actions of governments in intergovernmental organisations are thus open to interpretation along realist diplomatic lines. For a smaller power such as Britain, membership of these organisations is simply a way of gaining influence through involvement in a wider range of issues than would otherwise be possible. These organisations confer a new kind of power. This is the power to disrupt. The more transnational organisations are impregnated by state diplomacy, the less change they can initiate in world society. They may be saved from this ineffectual fate by the existence of the underlying phenomena to which they are addressed. The collapse of the IMF does not advance the solution of international monetary problems. The dangers of nuclear weapons are not lessened by failure to create security organisations. They may also be vitalised by the evolution of international languages which objectify the problems of the systems on which they are intended to operate. The language of international monetary economics is a cosmopolitan one in which the discussion of issues may proceed scientifically, though clearly it is a language which must take account of political realities. It is possible to detect the elements of an international language on the stable deployment of nuclear weapons, which has contributed to arms control agreements and which might develop further in the context of a new security organisation in Europe. Within the European Community there is a language of policy harmonisation, though it is not a widely used one.

The existence of the world of states is a constant threat to the validity of intergovernmental transnational organisations. The operational fact of statehood makes these organisations slow-moving entities, prone to search continuously for unanimity among their principal members. The policies of states may delimit the underlying systems to which they are addressed. The development of international languages relating to systemic problems may be delayed by ideological cleavages which correspond to state boundaries. States may attempt to use these organisations to further their narrower interests and thus convert them into arenas of power struggle. The world of states is thus a considerable impediment to the world of systemic control.

3. The institutions of world society do not fall into neat complementary relationships. Diplomacy establishes organisations and it may support them; but it may also ignore and undermine them. The tendency of small states to use the UN as a means of controlling the policies of larger states has led the latter to disregard much of the business transacted in the UN and to conduct their affairs through the traditional medium of diplomacy. The trade and monetary relations between the major Western countries are not conducted wholly in the context of the GATT and the IMF. Governments are commonly not averse to using extra-organisational means to press their interests if they can effectively do so. While diplomacy exists no international or transnational organisation at the governmental level can claim to enclose the international issues to which it is addressed. The United States recurrently shows impatience with the cumbrous apparatus of

the Community and is sometimes prone to stress a dominant diplomatic relationship with each of its members.

International institutional tensions are not restricted to the relations between diplomacy and formal organisations. Between organisations themselves there may be clashes of principle and practice. Though the Charter of the United Nations provides for the right of states to make regional defence arrangements, the continued existence of Nato contributes to the low standing of the UN in the very area, the authoritative maintenance of peace, where it was intended that it should make its greatest contribution. While the European Community makes preferential trading arrangements with specific outside countries, it harms the universal approach of the GATT to the removal of barriers to trade. Similarly, progress in one organisation may be impeded by a lack of progress in another. If, for example, the IMF were to be given the authority to make substantial special allocations of SDRs to underdeveloped countries, whose need to import capital goods tends otherwise to lead them into substantial balance of payments difficulties, little would be achieved if these countries could not then find markets for the products of their capital equipment because of the ineffectiveness of negotiations in the GATT. Nor do strategic and economic organisations occupy entirely separate compartments in world society. Developments in the European Community which appear to harm the economic interests of the United States may influence that country in further reducing its commitments to Nato, to the detriment of the defence interests of most EEC governments.

Britain is deeply involved in a variety of organisations and is thereby drawn into these problems of disharmony. A diplomacy which undermines organisations is unlikely to benefit a relatively small country which has little strength to deploy in the traditional arena of conflicting states. And foreign policy objectives which depend on the maintenance of organisations are not served if these organisations are weakened by their mutual tensions.

4. The paradoxes of the coexistence of two kinds of international environment reach a concentrated form in the European Community. This organisation develops transnationalism, private and governmental, among its constituent countries. Yet the transnational forces affecting any one of its members have their origins in a far wider environment than that which is marked by the boundaries of the Community. The direct legislative impact of the Community within constituent countries, the massive programme of harmonisation upon which it has

embarked, the existence of an active Community bureaucracy and of a Community Parliament, seem to point the Community as a whole towards the goal of a new statehood. Yet the constraints on the realisation of this goal are formidable. The depth of political commitment to the Community among its members, not least Britain, is uncertain. The decision-making process in the Community is markedly diplomatic in its constant search for unanimity in the Council of Ministers, though the internal nature of many of the subjects to which the Community addresses itself are markedly non-diplomatic. The powers of the European Parliament are slender. Yet increasing these powers means increasing the authority of the Community as a whole, and since this is likely to undermine the powers of national governments it is also likely to be resisted by many of them. While the European Parliament is weak, the diplomatic and bureaucratic nature of Community decision-making may seem an affront to democratic principles of popular participation and executive responsibility. The Community has no military competence, though its existence has strategic consequences. The Community attempts to act as a unit in international trade negotiations. There is a commitment among its governments that it should eventually do so in monetary matters as well. But the Community is not a diplomatic unit, though formal diplomatic consultations take place among its members. An intention of the Community is that it should add to the economic strength of its members. If this strength is used to support conflicting national foreign policies then the Community itself, as an economic and social unit, must be weakened. Yet in traditional terms the merging of national diplomacies implies the creation of a new state.

In occupying the territory between the world of states and the world of transnational systemic control, the EEC is subject to all the stresses and inconsistencies which these two worlds create. These stresses are implanted in the policies of the member governments, because, for the present, the future of the Community is in their hands. A major problem for each of them, and for all of them in conjunction, is the development of a coherent image of what the Community is and of what it is to become. This problem is central to British foreign policy in all its concerns, but it is also a problem which is deeply embedded in the substance of domestic policy and politics. Its existence is the most vivid manifestation of the changing structure of British foreign policy.

Part Two   The British situation

4 The strategic predicament

Britain retains small military forces in the non-European world. Looked at historically these establishments can be analysed as the vestiges of former world roles. Since Britain no longer has the internal strength to sustain these roles, it can be argued that its involvement in these distant theatres represents, at best, a harmless, though expensive, way of conducting largely theoretical military manœuvres. At worst, such commitments are hostages to fate. In a period of urgent crisis, these forces would be of negligible military assistance to friendly governments. Britain would be faced with the choice of sacrificing them, or withdrawing them with ignominious speed, or of reinforcing them and thus being drawn into heavy and quite unsustainable military and political exertions.

There are, from this general viewpoint, four defunct roles of which Britain's diminutive presence east of Suez is the remnant: first, the role of defender of the world's seaways, principally for British use; second, the role of preserver of the continued welfare and security of large British foreign investments, and of sources of raw materials vital to the operations of the British economy; third, the role of military aid, defender, and uniter of the Commonwealth countries; and, fourth, the role, particularly in the area of the Indian Ocean, of ally and deputy of the United States.

There are four familiar arguments to support the view that these roles are best forgotten. First, Britain does not have the naval strength to maintain the freedom of these vast seas if it were seriously threatened. Second, the future of British investments is largely dependent on political developments inside countries in which they are sited, and over these developments Britain can exercise no direct control and it would be fatal to her investments were she to forget this. Similarly, access to raw materials depends on indigenous political conditions and on Britain's ability to pay for what it needs: small military forces contribute nothing to the former and probably diminish the latter. Third, most Commonwealth governments do not want, or could not allow themselves to be seen to want, direct military assistance from a former colonial power. And, anyway, those Commonwealth countries which might, *in extremis*, need British military help would be assailed by forces too great for Britain to withstand. Fourth, the United States, after her prolonged distress in Indo-China, is not interested in the military services of a somewhat wayward lieutenant, though she might require a conveniently placed minor power to investigate dangerous situations, easily ignored if complications develop. Such a role has few advantages for the chosen minor power.

These are clearly strong arguments. An alternative view, which may result in similar conclusions, begins not by stressing existing dispositions in the context of the imperial past, but by asking two general questions: what are Britain's concerns in, say, the Indian Ocean area; and, second, what is the general place of external force in such an area?

Britain's fundamental concern has two aspects: that her own interests prosper, and that the international milieu should be a stable and peaceful one. To these ends it is important that international investment in the Third World should grow and be as secure as possible, that trade should also grow, and that governments and peoples should have as much peace and freedom as possible to work out political forms to which they can attach value and relevance in a general setting which does not lead them to regard the West as their collective enemy.

These liberal concerns are broadly shared by Western Europe, and by the West at large, and they are concerns which reflect a civilised regard for the future of indigenous populations in relatively poor parts of the world. It is probably the case that many poor countries generally have before them prolonged prospects of internal disorders. Similarly there are regional international conflicts (in the Persian Gulf, in Southeast Asia and the East Indies, for example) whose complications and confusions stretch far into the future. But prospects such as these, it may be contended, do not alter the long-term interests of Britain.

DIRECT AND INDIRECT POLICIES

There are two 'pure' forms of outside military intrusion: assistance in the form of armaments and advice; and intervention by military forces under outside command. The former is currently provided widely by industrialised countries and presumably will continue to be so. As a form of intervention rather than a form of trade it has several advantages for the donor. It may assist a client government. It may tilt or maintain a regional international balance in a way considered desirable. At the same time it does not have an inbuilt tendency to draw the donor into embroilment in complicated local situations, though it does give him some leverage on the recipient. The disadvantages are that a military capability conferred in the form of arms may be used by a decidedly illiberal government not to maintain a desired external balance but to repress internal liberal movements. Similarly, military assistance given with too free a hand may encourage rulers to exaggerate their strength and to act with dangerous flamboyance on the local international stage. Nor does the supply of this kind of assistance necessarily confer anything like decisive political influence on the donor, as both first-rank powers have at times discovered in the Middle East.

Military forces stationed on a specific territory have some advantages from the viewpoint of their own governments. They are a concrete means of supporting a government or a local international *status quo*. They offer a means of apparently clear action in confused local circumstances, because of their capacity for disciplined response to instructions from their own authorities. They are a means of injecting foreign exchange and purchasing power into the host territory. More important, they can be a token of a strong commitment, behind which may lie the threat of the use of nuclear weapons, though these weapons are not thereby placed at the disposal of local rulers.

Experiences of the postwar world have tended to cause the disadvantages of this kind of direct military pressure to be more vividly appreciated than the advantages. A physical presence can create an intense commitment to maintain conditions which turn out to be locally unacceptable, and instead of conferring power over local events on the external government it tends to transfer power from the external site to some internal leader or faction. In this kind of way the external government may cease to be a mover of events and be more nearly dominated by them. Nor is the remote threat of the use of nuclear weapons much help in a situation where few believe their use to be likely or relevant. An incredible threat is a useless one, both militarily and politically.

The first-rank powers, particularly the Soviet Union, have come to appreciate the merits of indirect intervention through military aid, principally in the form of supplies, and direct presence, not necessarily intervention, in the form of naval forces. A navy has indirect qualities which render it suitable to deployment in complex and sensitive political circumstances. It operates on a relatively unpolitical element, the sea. As a military unit a naval force is remarkably mobile and self-contained, and modern developments have rendered it almost as independent of local base facilities as such forces were in Nelson's day, and now, of course, a navy can deploy immense strategic firepower.

Advantages such as these have led to a great stress on the role of external sea power in the Third World. But there is a great deal sea power cannot do. It cannot occupy territory, it cannot engage effectively in even modest land battles, and it is of only marginal use in a long campaign against subversion. It can mount a bombardment, execute a *coup de main*, threaten sea lanes, maintain a blockade, manifest the existence of a nuclear threat. But it is not well suited to the exercise of long-term control over political events.

In a sense, the increasing international presence of naval units controlled by totalitarian governments constitutes a threat to all forms of sea transport. But the circumstances which would lead a government of the Soviet Union to attempt to cut sea lanes in, say, the Indian Ocean, thus isolating sources of important materials from Western Europe and Japan, could be little short of total world war. If the prospect of total war is unacceptable to the Soviet Union the danger to the West must be largely a symbolic one, a sense of pressure creating a nervous sense of vulnerability.

The role of sea power in relation to indigenous governments in underdeveloped countries is similarly indistinct, yet not thereby negligible. A symbol of power might, in some circumstances, tilt the general trend of policies in ways unfavourable to Western interests.

It is important, one might argue, that a Communist naval presence should not be allowed to exercise a monopoly, even a symbolic one. In this sense, British naval activity in Third World oceans, on however reduced a scale, may be held to confer general benefits. It is, as it were, a political gesture, important in a number of senses. First, it is a token of European strength, basically economic but potentially military. Second, it is a token of European worldwide interests and involvements. Third, it is a token that the West is not a monolith but a group of likeminded but dissimilar peoples. In this way it could soften the image of the West as an American-dominated clique, an image which is harmful to the long-term interests of the United States and the West generally. Fourth, by serving an interest which is also, in general terms, the interest of Japan, it helps to draw that powerful country into the Western community. Perhaps, in a minor way, it thus helps to maintain the economic emphasis of Japan's foreign relations, and reduces pressures on that country to acquire a massive military capability. Fifth, to the degree (which may, of course, be negligible) that a measure of military display, naval and otherwise, inhibits the growth of isolationism in Australia and New Zealand and encourages those countries to play an increasing liberal role in their region, possibly in general association with Japan, then a creative purpose is served. Sixth, if British exertions reduce the feeling of American governments that they labour alone under the burden and obloquy of sustaining Western interests in the world at large, and that they might as well withdraw to their own fortress, then this too might be interpreted as a modest reward.

It cannot be forgotten that a British presence, however slender and symbolic, loses any conviction as a strategic deterrent without a sense of American involvement. So while it may be important that differences of policy between the United States and Britain (over relations between India and Pakistan, for example) should be seen to exist, it is also important that there should be no sense of strain over the Anglo-American sense that a liberal world order is what present travails are about. This pursuit requires a punctilious regard for the form of the state in most underdeveloped areas, virtually regardless of its reality. For the form of the state has been a limitation on conflict and a bar to external intrusions, which, though in the past it has been little appreciated, serves ultimate Western interests. And the loose association of nuclear strength with international problems everywhere has a dampening effect on interstate conflicts, though not on intrastate conflicts.

All these purposes of a British military presence in the non-European world, despite its costs, dangers, and embarrassments, may be argued to make it worthwhile. But the extent to which Britain actually furthers these purposes by her slender military deployments is obviously marginal. This very marginality must make complete British withdrawal to the European theatre an imminent possibility.

What is potentially more than marginal is the possible British role on the non-military plane. In Western Europe, Britain is part of what is potentially one of the largest economic markets in the world. It is also a market far more concerned, proportionately, with overseas trade than either the Soviet Union or the United States. In the same way, Western Europe is far more heavily dependent on externally supplied materials, particularly oil, than either of the first-rankers. In these circumstances, which combine great economic potential with great economic weakness, it is arguably an important British concern to move Western Europe towards an indulgent foreign economic policy and to change its image as a group of selfish wealth-seekers.

It is unlikely that other European governments will ever openly contribute to British military exertions in a non-European area such as the Indian Ocean. They might, however, be persuaded to see them in a favourable light. But whatever the future of military involvements, the main concern of British foreign policy towards the non-European world is likely to fall in the area of foreign economic policy, and in this area, if successive British governments remain committed to the Community programme, she will cease to have a foreign policy of her own in the traditional sense. So one might contend that it is foreign economic policy which gives meaning to foreign military policy in the present context, and the foreign economic policy in question is centrally that of the Community, not Britain alone. This is the way in which the nature of overseas strategy, traditionally an area of high national policy, thrusts Britain into the mundane intricacies of European politics, where the distinction between the internal and the external dissolves and the pursuit of a definite line of overall policy becomes as difficult as it is normally expected to be in a pluralist domestic arena.

British influence on external European economic policy is likely to depend upon the degree to which Britain succeeds in integrating herself into the Community. But the more integrated her economy the greater will be the voice of internal European economic interests on external European policy; and the greater the voice of sectional and industrial interests the slower and more rigid policy-making is likely to become, and the less enlightened, perhaps, its concern with the rest of the world. Similarly, the economic strain of adjusting to integration into the Community, coupled with internal British infirmities, may well force British governments to press their partners for indulgent and preferential policies towards Britain itself, so distracting attention from wider international duties, and, anyway, very much reducing the British stature in European counsels.

THE EUROPEAN THEATRE

In Europe, an expressly nuclear theatre, matters of immediate strategic practice must loom larger than in the extra-European theatre. Without safety in Europe there can be no role at all for Britain in the rest of the world. In Europe British governments are likely to remain concerned with defence through the maintenance of a balance of deterrence such that the Soviet Union cannot exert intense military pressure on any Western European country. British governments may also be concerned with the creation of a security system in Europe, a more complex goal which depends upon the development of an environment in which emphasis on defence becomes less pressing. The pursuit of these two goals of defence and security, often contradictory in their immediate demands on governments, constitutes the theme of the rest of this chapter.

THE NEGATIVE RESPONSE

There is an extreme answer to the complexities of involvement in defence and security: Britain could assert its sovereignty and withdraw from all its alliances and abandon all its armaments.

Such a course raises a number of moral questions. Britain has assumed specific military obligations: to assist its North Atlantic Treaty allies; to maintain armed forces in the Federal Republic of Germany; to perform military duties which the United Nations may require of it. The abandonment of international contracts such as these is clearly not punishable at law, but this does not affect their moral standing. From the viewpoint of the search for safety through security, it is a somewhat inconsistent argument which holds that a world of binding contracts and obligations can in any way be brought nearer by the abandonment of present obligations.

Assuming, however, that scruples could be overcome and the unfavourable reactions of offended governments (in other areas, economic perhaps) endured, what kind of strategic policies could be served by such a resort? First, it might be contended that actions such as these need not serve any policy but highminded revulsion from all things military. After withdrawal, Britain's impact on strategy, European and otherwise, would be that of a moral observer, influencing events in the arena by its comments and, possibly, by its good offices. The effectiveness of such a role is questionable. Good offices are already in plentiful supply. And those engaged in the perplexing detail of serious but unpleasant policies tend to find observations on the part of the disengaged irrelevant, annoying, and contemptible in their claims to superior moral status.

Second, there is the grandiose, but equally moralistic, policy of example. By the total abnegation of all military relationships, Britain could set a shining example which all other countries would follow. This is a view which probably wildly exaggerates the position of Britain in world society. Other countries do not necessarily defer to the British as superior moral beings. If other countries do not follow this example nothing is achieved in the environment and any hope of changing the nature of international society, in however minor a fashion, must be largely abandoned.

Third, there is the rather more honest, though selfish and amoral policy of securing defence for Britain at no cost. A disarmed and non-participating Britain is still anchored off the coast of Western Europe. The United States and other European countries would remain committed to a defence system which would have the byproduct of providing safety for Britain, whose governments would be put to no trouble or expense thereby. This policy relies on the surrounding alliance to hold together and to remain liberal. In its nature this is a policy which sacrifices any positive role in maintaining these conditions; yet these are the conditions which give the policy its point. In the same way, Britain would be excluded from direct participation in constructing a security system.

A second conceivable course involving the extreme renewal of traditional state sovereignty would be for Britain to abandon the troublesome life of alliances and adopt a completely independent role, but one founded on an exclusively national military capability. A primary difficulty here is the nature of the capability which Britain could maintain. To develop first-class nuclear strength would cause domestic economic and political strains which few governments in anything approaching normal international circumstances could contemplate. To maintain a military capability of the present modest order in isolation would involve an extra military effort, because a part of Britain's nuclear capability (currently the most modern part of it) is imported from the United States, whose governments might be disinclined to continue this form of trade.

Given that this deficiency in domestic supply could be overcome, what policy could be attached to a military capability of roughly contemporary dimensions? The possibilities mentioned in connection with the spectacle of a disarmed Britain would remain open, but if one or more of these were adopted military capability would be irrelevant anyway. There is also the alternative of the policy of pure defence of the homeland from military attack, or pressure based on a capacity for attack. But it requires little argument to show that the British Isles are totally vulnerable to nuclear attack and that a nuclear capability of the contemporary British order has a low deterrence potential. In any major conflict with a first-rank power a British government would be faced with the choice between abject surrender or virtual suicide. It would have little chance of adapting a major opponent's position by pressure. In a less serious conflict, a British government would have a minor deterrence capability in the sense that it could inflict a punishment on its opponent, at immense possible cost, which its opponent might be reluctant to risk in the context of a minor quarrel. This small and uncertain capability is conferred on Britain by the decision of the first-rank powers to limit their antimissile defences. If the first-rankers were to abandon this policy, a minor nuclear power such as Britain would be virtually devoid of deterrence capability since all its weapons could be prevented from reaching their targets. Similarly, an isolated Britain would be unable to brandish the strength of allies, since she would have none. She would also be less able to benefit from fears that a nuclear exchange with herself could somehow trigger a larger nuclear war involving both the first-rank powers, for both these would almost certainly find their interests coinciding to a degree sufficient to underpin effective joint arrangements to prevent catastrophe being thrust upon them in this way by an isolated and irresponsible minor power.

If Britain's military capability looks inadequate to sustain a fortress policy of home defence, how could it contribute notably to the creation of a European security system? In its nature, such a system must be the product of widely collective effort. But non-participation in alliance politics would rule out Britain as a direct influence on other powers from the outset.

EUROPEAN ALTERNATIVES

By a process of eliminating other possibilities, if by no other route, we come to the conclusion that Britain is likely to remain a member of a defence alliance. Given this to be so, there is a further hypothetical course which may be profitably discussed. This is the possibility of Britain becoming a part of an exclusively Western European defence bloc dissociated from the United States.

Such an alliance would be attended by a number of hazards and contradictions. There would be little point to it if it were unable to offer a convincing deterrent threat towards its formidable first-rank

neighbour, the Soviet Union. In European conditions, where industrial and population concentrations are high, where room for military
manœuvre is exceedingly limited, and where there is virtually no
scope for territorial concessions to an enemy, a Western European
military alliance would logically be required to adopt a strategy of
flexible response, with substantial conventional forces distributed near
its sensitive borders and supported, militarily and psychologically, by
a full range of nuclear weapons.

With very substantial United States contributions, Nato does not
deploy a thoroughly convincing capability of this kind. So the first and
most obvious difficulty which a purely European alliance would have
to face would be the necessity for increased military effort simply to
maintain conventional force levels. Expenditure does not solve all
military manpower problems. There might be a pressing need for the
renewal of compulsory military service. The internal political difficulty of such a course need not be emphasised.

Additional to the need for a greater exertion in the matter of conventional forces, there would be the necessity for building up a first-
class nuclear capability to carry deterrent conviction at both the
tactical and strategic levels. If the second-class European countries pro-
ceeded as at present, the European capability would be simply the
distinct capabilities of Britain and France. Jointly or separately, these
forces do not comprise a formidable deterrent at the first-rank level.

The political consequences of the existence of a totally inadequate
deterrent force in Western Europe could be serious. West Germany,
for example, would be pushed towards either of two contrary positions. First, she could step up her own military efforts, both in conventional and nuclear terms, to compensate for the weakness of her
allies and to insure against their possible irresolution in a crisis. This
course would ignore the treaty provisions which currently obligate
Germany not to acquire nuclear weapons. More significantly, it would
alarm the Soviet Union and its East German ally, causing them to
adopt a more intransigent stance in their approach to European
problems. Efforts to ease relations with Eastern Europe could thus be
negated. In this kind of way, the creation of a purely European alliance
might create the very situation of intense military threat which it
would least be capable of confronting. A second policy available to
West Germany would be to alter its political alignment, abandon the
European alliance and lean towards the East. This would deprive the
European alliance of its most substantial national economy, and trans-

form it into a disconnected string of states on the fringe of Europe, each liable to overwhelming pressure from the East.

In these imagined circumstances of an independent Western Europe, the creation of an effective European security system would be removed to the level of illusion. The Soviet Union and her allies would have no real need for such a system, being secure in their European dominance.

An alternative path for this hypothetical Western European bloc would be the merging of national forces into a fully integrated European army backed by an entirely coherent first-class nuclear capability. In purely economic terms, there can be no doubt that such a course is within the material capacity of Western Europe as a whole. However, the political difficulties remain formidable. Treaty obligations would still constitute a hindrance to full participation in a joint nuclear effort by the German Federal Republic. As before, if this reticence were overcome the consequent deterioration in European relations might be formidable, and formidably dangerous during the gestation of the new nuclear force.

A second set of obstacles might be caused by French attitudes. In recent years, French governments have taken the view that the state remains the fundamental unit of world society and that the essential quality of the state resides in its sovereign control over the use of force. Consequently, though France has remained bound by the North Atlantic Treaty, its armed forces have been removed from the Nato command structure. Though this policy need not be immutable, it clearly corresponds to some of the basic forces making up the French political system, and its logic, given its premises, would apply as much, even more, to the prospect of an integrated European force as it has applied to the fairly pliable arrangements of Nato.

A third set of difficulties would be caused by the nature of Western Europe. This is not a group of countries with uniform attitudes towards the place of military force in relation to themselves and in relation to Europe generally. Norway, for example, does not allow foreign troops to be stationed on its territory. Italy has major internal movements antipathetic to Nato, and generally Italian governments play their role in Europe in a very low key. Norway is not a member of EEC, Ireland is a member of EEC but not of Nato. And so on. The creation of a European force, if it were to have any conviction, would have to bring Britain, France and Western Germany together in a union so tight as to constitute the creation of a new first-rank state.

Overlooking the formidable difficulty of this enterprise, it would still be true that this new state would exist in a welter of confusing connections with the other European countries which could constitute an extremely difficult field of political operations.

Fourthly, the progress of political integration in EEC has been very slow. There is no reason to believe that it would be any faster in a new European defence community. But in this case the need for unified political control would be vastly greater and there might be no available time to allow for a long evolutionary process. In the meantime a political halfway house would be far more dangerous in the military than in the economic field. Opportunities for exploiting political disunity during the run-up of military unpreparedness might prove an intense temptation to a Soviet government anxious to prevent the rise of another first-class state on its European borders, which, together with the rise of China in the East might induce a totally undesirable and counterproductive sense of encircled desperation in the Soviet Union.

An independent Western European defence bloc would be a highly imperfect political and defence entity. Only one condition capable of generating such a bloc comes reasonably to mind: the complete withdrawal of the United States into an exclusively national defence policy. A change of this kind, though it may occur, is unlikely to be to the advantage of the United States. It would place Western Europe in an unstable situation, and the collapse of so wealthy and so broadly friendly a set of countries would reduce the stature of the United States in the world at large, and would harm the fabric of world trade and world political relations to which American interests and values are committed. An American government of liberal outlook is unlikely to be eager to remove itself entirely from Europe as a matter of purely unilateral policy.

Alternatively, the United States could be thrust into such a policy by the recalcitrance of the Europeans themselves. But for many signatories of the North Atlantic Treaty a prime necessity of strategic policy is the avoidance of this kind of situation. For example, a basis of West German policies of detente towards the East has been the strength provided by the background presence of the United States. The government of the Federal Republic has not been required to negotiate from weakness. At the same time there has been no question of its flaunting its own military strength. This delicate conjunction of weakness and strength is the foundation of West German policies and it is unlikely that an ordinary German government would willingly destroy it. Similarly, Britain's strategy since 1940 has been founded on the necessity of involving the United States intimately in the military affairs of Europe. Even French governments have realised that their own strategic endeavours lose much of both their military and political significance removed entirely from the context of the North Atlantic Treaty.

Thus, by a process of elimination if by no other, one comes to the conclusion that the basic problems of British strategy are the problems of living within the Atlantic alliance. It is, of course, true that Nato might collapse and that British governments should make some kind of provision, be it only intellectual, for this eventuality. But their main concern is likely to be with the maintenance of Nato, and they are likely to contemplate a strategic future without the American connection with gloom and revulsion.

THE ATLANTIC ALLIANCE

Pursuing our basic distinction, British governments have two basic strategic concerns in Europe: the maintenance of defence and the pursuit of security. These goals are simple neither in themselves nor in their relationship. In the nuclear age defence in Europe must mean deterrence in Europe. The logic of deterrence presses the Atlantic alliance into a strategy of flexible response, with its emphasis on conventional forces deployed in ways not entirely dissimilar to the defensive modes of prenuclear times. In this setting a concern for defence, a concern for safety and the maintenance of the *status quo*, must be equated with a concern for the credibility of deterrence. If the deterrent is credible it should not be put to the test. If the deployment of force becomes unbalanced in some way (by the excessive rundown of conventional forces, for example) then the system becomes unstable because the threat loses an element of credibility and in a crisis an opponent might be able to exert psychological pressure or might even be tempted to launch an attack.

A concern for security, on the other hand, might be interpreted as the desire to create international conditions conducive to a state of psychological ease and safety sufficient to allow a relaxation of defence. Defence pursued through deterrence cannot in its nature provide safety because it is ultimately dedicated to the attack, not to blocking the attack. In a completely secure environment there would be no cause to pursue defence at all. But where there is real international conflict there cannot be a completely secure environment, because states can defy international arrangements and organisations.

In fact safety through deterrence is highly imperfect. And any realistically conceived system of security must be highly imperfect too. It is because of this basic imperfection that both policies can be pursued at once. A total relaxation of defence and an equally total concentration on security is a disastrous choice if security proves to be illusory. But, conversely, a complete neglect of security is conducive to the intensification of distrust and hostility between the parties in conflict; this is conducive to an arms race; an arms race is conducive to instability in deterrence; and a breakdown of deterrence in war destroys everyone's safety, which the policy of defence is supposed to preserve.

The first-rank powers have a mutual interest in agreeing to some control of armaments in order to reduce the chances of an inadvertent or desperate military outburst and to economise on military expenditure. The formal pursuit of arms control necessarily pushes the first-rankers some way towards the pole of security, but the closer they approach that pole the greater become the risks of bad faith, political misunderstandings and unbalanced, and consequently unstable, run-downs of military capability. Additionally, the closer they approach the pole of security, the greater the extent of political contacts between the parties and the greater the degree of mutual political dependence. In the nature of things, increasingly close contact between parties with different values and outlooks is not necessarily conducive to complete harmony between them; perhaps the reverse. Moving from the pursuit of defence to the pursuit of security is likely to be a slow business. A long coexistence of both policies must be expected.

General issues of defence and security manifest themselves in a number of international negotiations affecting the European theatre. At the level of the first-rankers there is a continuing series of bilateral negotiations on the limitation of strategic arms. Still in the military field, but at a multilateral level including both first-rankers and other members of Nato and the Warsaw Pact, there are negotiations on mutual force reductions in Europe. And in the generalised political security field, at a level including almost all the European states, there are talks on security and cooperation in Europe. Disarmament is widely discussed outside these three principal negotiations, notably in the Geneva disarmament conference. Small groups of Western allies have negotiated with the USSR over specific issues, notably over the status of Berlin. And individual Western powers can take up the pursuit of security; most outstandingly Western Germany has done so in her *ostpolitik*. But the three principal sets of negotiations mentioned above, together with the general issues they raise, are likely to be the backdrop to the future pursuit of defence and security in Europe.

British governments are committed to defence through deterrence, and they have a clear concern that deterrence should be stable. They are therefore involved in the practical strategy of flexible response. This strategy, as we have seen, requires the maintenance of conventional forces backed by tactical nuclear weapons, the whole resting on the deterrent base of a secure strategic intercontinental capability. In Europe, essential ingredients at each of these three levels are provided by the United States. American governments contribute substantially to Nato conventional forces. The United States provides the mass of tactical nuclear weapons. Except for the small, integrated British capability and the small, unintegrated French capability, the United States provides the foundation of ultimate strategic nuclear capability.

This central role of an extra-European power in the defence of Western Europe creates a number of related uncertainties, of which two are outstanding. Would the United States actually use her capability in dire crisis in Europe? And, second, is the United States likely to make bilateral arrangements with the Soviet Union which could be harmful to the stability of Europe?

In the nature of the case, these questions do not have certain answers. The most that a British government pursuing defence can do is to act in such a way as to keep uncertainty within tolerable bounds, so that the risks facing an aggressor in Europe are sufficiently high to deter him. What is at issue is the credibility of deterrence. If deterrence loses its credibility the balance becomes unstable and the whole defence apparatus might be put to the test. A successful, a credible, deterrent is not put to the test, in terms of either psychological or direct military pressure. British defence depends on a deterrent working effectively in Europe.

Though committed to Nato, most tactical nuclear weapons in Europe remain ultimately in American hands. Arrangements for handing them over to Europeans in dire emergency depend on unilateral American decision. At this pivot of defence, the credibility of the deterrent in Europe manifestly depends on the policies of the government of the United States. It also depends on American deployment of conventional military forces, because if United States troops are not to be intimately and violently involved in any incident which occurs, doubts are likely to grow as to whether a United States government would, in the event, feel under pressure to use its nuclear capability, given the risk of dire consequences for itself which use might bring. If American troops are not deployed, graduated nuclear deterrence loses credibility. The backstop to graduated deterrence is the threat of massive retaliation. But, as indicated above, it was just the incredibility of massive retaliation which led to the development of graduated deterrence and flexible response.

American troops in Europe comprise a substantial part of the physical mass necessary to a policy of flexible response. In terms of the size of Soviet conventional capabilities in Eastern Europe, European forces available for flexible response along the borders of Nato powers most at risk are far from adequate. The rundown of these forces tends to move their function towards the largely passive one of being a trip-wire, concerned largely with activating a somewhat problematic nuclear response. There is thus an effective argument that the structure of allied strategy in Europe depends on the maintenance of American troop commitments.

However, American governments are likely to be under continued economic and political pressure to reduce overseas establishments generally. An emphasis is therefore being laid upon the reinforcement capability of the United States: substantial air transport capacity is allocated to the task of physically moving troops from the United States to Europe in periods of crisis. The effect of this policy, if taken very far, is to place the whole structure even more at the unilateral disposal of American governments. In a crisis, the transportation of large troop reserves could hardly be accomplished secretly, and the whole operation could take the form of an overt mobilisation roughly along taditional lines. The military efficacy of such a manœuvre is doubtful because troops suddenly placed in strange terrain labour under a grave disadvantage. Its political problems are even more significant. In time of crisis mobilisation may seem a very crude instrument, more likely to exacerbate tensions than to relieve them. In these circumstances an American government must be under severe pressure not to act in this way. And an adversary is capable of appreciating the existence of this pressure, of acting on it, and of thus undermining the deterrent structure on which defence depends.

Neither a British government nor any other European government is likely to gain direct access to American–Soviet negotiations on strategic arms control. Hitherto these negotiations have concentrated on stabilising the intercontinental strategic capabilities of these countries. So long as these negotiations remain at this kind of level, European governments are not heavily affected, since the United States government is likely to be quite as concerned as they are to maintain the credibility of the American strategic deterrent. In the remote event that these negotiations began to concentrate on actually reducing the intercontinental nuclear capabilities of these two first-class powers, Western European defence might be adversely affected, since in Europe the USSR has the military advantages of larger conventional military forces and of internal lines of communication (she does not have to cross an ocean to get to central Europe). The USSR is thus better placed to issue a challenge in Europe in general circumstances of reduced deterrence.

For this reason, British and Western European governments must be sensitive to the defence implications of any arrangements affecting the military capabilities of the first-class powers. The British defence interest requires that as many negotiations as possible bearing on the deterrence system should take place at a multilateral level where Western European voices may be heard. But the dangers of arms limitations agreements at the first-rank level also appear at the European level. The specific problems of arms reductions in Europe are legion. Should reductions be confined to a particular area in Europe? Should restrictions apply to conventional or nuclear arms, or both? Should there be naval reductions? Given the slim geography of Western Europe, the emphasis of Nato on sea power, its cumbersome structure, its relatively small land forces and its dependence on the United States, the balance of defence advantage in negotiation and agreement on these topics may seem to lie wholly with the Soviet Union. There may therefore be a tendency among Europeans to see a defence danger at every negotiation on arms control in Europe. But this attitude could be a defence danger in itself. The sheer tardiness and suspicion of Western Europeans could have the effect of pushing this whole subject up into the stratum where first-rank powers negotiate directly and exclusively, and where the defence interests of Europeans might be neglected.

In these circumstances British defence policy is likely to continue to emphasise the close mutual commitment and dependence of the United States and Western Europe. Solidarity in Nato and caution in approaching strategic change have become established themes in

British foreign policy. A member of an alliance particularly concerned with its coherence is likely to do its utmost to placate its most powerful partner, in this case the United States. Yet the United States stresses the value of Western European self-help, and is concerned to reduce American military burdens. British governments are therefore likely to be aware of a need to maintain their contributions to Nato forces, in the context of likely American force reductions. The need to make the most of military budgets is likely to compel Britain to continue along the tedious technical path of promoting standardisation of European military equipment. Even if this does not prove outstandingly economical it nevertheless knits the alliance together in innumerable practical ways. Similarly, British governments are likely to be active, as the United States desires them to be, in expressly European consultations on Western strategy, and this concern has manifested itself tentatively in British participation in the 'Eurogroup' within Nato. At the same time French governments must be cultivated at relatively informal levels because European strategic policies which exclude France are hardly European.

A position which stresses the European responsibility in European defence is immersed in a basic ambiguity. If European governments signally fail to integrate their policies or to assume greater burdens, perhaps in economic rather than military terms, the long-term effect on the United States could be unfavourable to the Euro-American strategic connection. On the other hand, if the core European countries were to integrate too effectively and to become formidably assertive in their own right, this too could have a destructive effect on the American connection. Caught between these poles, British governments are likely to remain subject to the charge of being bad and devious Europeans, at one moment urging European integration, at the next truckling to the twists of American politics. This old balancing act is complemented by another, more obvious perhaps to outsiders: if other Western European countries were to succumb to extremist politics Britain would have to resort to the old Anglo-Saxon alliance for defence; in the same sort of way, if the United States withdrew once again into isolationism or became overclose in her relations with the Soviet Union, Britain would see the case for an even more profound kind of integration in Europe than has hitherto seemed desirable or possible.

Improbable though outcomes such as these may seem, they must constitute some of the defence considerations to be weighed as eventual obsolescence raises the question of the future of Britain's small nuclear deterrent. If this force is allowed to wither away, Britain would have little to bring to a Europe abandoned by the United States. She might have to revert to an earlier, not entirely happy, role of submitting to the continental military leadership of France. A British government which decides to refurbish the nuclear deterrent unassisted by the United States or anyone else, is likely to expose itself to charges of wasteful sentimentality for first-rank status: nor would such a course seem to serve any useful alliance purpose because Britain's nuclear force would still be a second-class one, albeit up to date, which would be incapable of deterring a first-ranker on behalf of an ally. If, alternatively, Britain moves into a new generation of nuclear weapons with the assistance of the United States (assuming this to be as forthcoming in the future as it has been in the past, which is far from certain) she does so cheaply. But, in doing so, she distinguishes herself from her European allies in an Anglo-Saxon way and does nothing to integrate Western Europe or to absorb French nuclear potential into a European design.

There may thus be a motivation to join in a weapons development programme in partnership with France. Supposing a French government were agreeable to this course, such a prospect still summons visions of Anglo-French tensions beside which difficulties in the construction of the Concorde aircraft pale into mediocrity. How far should new developments be taken? What level of expenditure could be agreed to? Would the two powers move jointly into the tactical nuclear field? How would developments such as these affect arms control in Europe? How would a nuclear defence system jointly developed be deployed? A joint weapons development programme which was unaccompanied by political and military integration would add to the military capability of France while conferring very little influence over French policies. Integration, were it to prove possible, might, on the other hand, draw Britain into French strategic individualism, thus raising all the problems associated with an over-confident assertion of European military capability. All this would again raise the dangerous question of the status and nuclear contribution of Western Germany.

INTERNATIONAL SECURITY

A conceptual distinction has been drawn throughout this essay between the pursuit of defence and the pursuit of security. In practice these two concerns are closely but ambiguously related.

The pursuit of defence usually reflects a sense of danger, of insecurity. Yet the pursuit of security may be held to be dependent on defence because no true negotiation on specific causes of tension is possible from a position of weakness. This attitude has been fundamental to allied negotiations with the East, on, for example, the status of Berlin, and a similar attitude has informed the German Federal Republic's Eastern policies. To require conciliatory policies from an opponent in an international setting, and to offer conciliatory policies oneself, is commonly held to be a function of strength not weakness. Negotiation from weakness can only take the form of appeasement. So it is argued that security in Europe is pursued, first, by the maintenance of adequate armed forces; second, by negotiation on very specific issues, such as Berlin; and, third, by the search for a stable balance of armaments.

There is also a fourth path, which is to discuss very general political problems of security in a multilateral setting where the future of the Continent may be contemplated and general political principles formulated to bring it to a condition of wellbeing. A number of difficulties attend endeavours of this very general kind. First, it is a familiarly British standpoint which suspects the efficacy of the general, particularly in international relations, where a future crisis of interests will pay scant regard to highminded principles of the past. Second, the formulation of generalities in international relations is rarely disinterested, and an examination of the possible motivations of the Soviet Union in relation to European stability and security may not be conducive to the desired feelings of security. The sceptical may feel, for example, that Soviet governments are concerned to obtain Western recognition of the complete legitimacy of their empire in Eastern Europe while simultaneously encouraging a lax approach by the Western allies to the European arms balance and to the maintenance of Nato solidarity, all in return for high-sounding generalities. Third, generalities referring to Europe as a whole may have a strong emotional impact on subject peoples whose freedom may largely exist only at a psychological level. A British policy in Europe is a European policy, and Europe contains peoples to the East who are subject to the control of Soviet governments whose regard for the quality of European civilisation is unenlightened. To pursue security at the cost of psychologically abandoning subject peoples might be held to be a renewal of appeasement in an undramatic but corrupting form. In the long run, the liberal governments of Western Europe cannot morally be *status quo* powers.

From a defence viewpoint, it is likely to remain a primary British concern that the United States should be fully committed to the protection of Western Europe. To this end it is also likely to be a British concern to nurture and sustain the institutions of Nato, both as a means of continuing the American involvement in Europe and as a means of maintaining Western European influence upon United States governments anxious to reduce their overseas defence establishments and inclined to draw strategically closer to the Soviet Union.

But Britain stands to gain more, in terms of increased safety, from a secure environment in Europe. Part of Britain's predicament is that she must be concerned with the environmental goal of security without abandoning the limited measure of safety conferred by the policy of defence in the context of the deterrent strength of Nato. It is the function of politics to reconcile particular demands and general interests, and a commitment to politics is a commitment to the national and international possibility of this kind of reconciliation. From the standpoint of this commitment, it is the ultimate strategic-political task of British governments to contribute to the creation of general institutions of European security without destroying defence and without losing their coolness towards purely verbal formulas.

Multilateral negotiations on arms limitation and arms balance in Europe are likely to be prolonged. They might well form the basis for the establishment of a permanent European Security Organisation. The purpose of such an organisation would not primarily be to negotiate a series of specific treaties on arms limitations, the weaknesses of which were sketched in an earlier chapter, but to develop a working system of security. An organisation of this kind would have to contain the first-rank powers. Without them its deliberations would be empty, and its impact on the overall problems of safety, in nuclear terms, negligible. But such an organisation would offer the prospect of a new and creative role for lesser governments such as those of Britain. The development of a common style of discourse within the new European Security Organisation could form the basis of a practical measure of international inspection of military installations in specific areas of Eastern and Western Europe. The next step might be the tentative commitment of some European military forces, including some of those of Britain, to the new organisation. And so on: gradually the organisation could move from the development of a common outlook on security problems to the acquisition and command of military forces capable, ultimately, of enforcing security. In the long intermediate period the role of relatively minor powers such as Britain could be central.

Taking a lead in such a programme would be a task presenting Britain with a number of difficulties. In the past, British governments have not been notable for their pioneering zeal in the creation of transnational European organisations. A new organisation dealing with disposition of military forces, traditionally a matter at the core of national sovereignty, would be too bold a project to be congenial to traditionalist strains of opinion in Britain. Among many international difficulties, such a project might not be at all agreeable to French governments, though it might be approved by American governments moving towards general detente with the Soviet Union: so by furthering such an organisation, Britain might once again appear to be placing the interests of the United States before those of France. More importantly in the long run perhaps, a scheme of European security intimately involving the United States and the Soviet Union is the negation of the possibility of a group within the European Community becoming a new first-rank military power. If Community territory, or parts of its territory, are to be open to international military inspection, if parts of the military forces of its members are to be assigned to an international organisation whose membership would include the existing first-rankers and the states of Eastern Europe, then the creation of a new first-rank national sovereignty in Western Europe would be out of the question.

However, the benefits of new European Security Organisation would render it a hopeful way forward through the moral and security dilemmas of the strategic environment. It might contribute to the emancipation of the Eastern European countries through their political participation in its deliberations and through their military contributions to its forces. It would lay the foundations of an international security system which might in time extend its competence to the territories and forces of the first-rank powers. In its initial competence it need not be hopelessly ambitious. By its involvement of the United States and the Soviet Union it would be anchored in the harsh realities of deterrence in the nuclear age. Similarly, in its beginnings it need offer no fundamental threat to Nato, which would provide the confidence necessary for the smaller powers to fulfil a creative European role. In its later stages the techniques and even the machinery of Nato, being transnational, might blend successfully with the new organisation. In this way the large theoretical problem of reconciling the demands of defence and security might begin to be solved in attention to the practical details of transnational military inspection and the commitment of military forces to the new machinery. This allocation of forces in the earlier stages need not be an unrealistic course for lesser governments because provision would have to exist for speedy national withdrawal of forces should circumstances, as determined by individual governments, so require; and the canopy of nuclear deterrence and first-rank involvement in Europe would be untouched.

The physical dangers of the existence of nuclear armaments, together with the political rigidity, in terms of the maintenance of the *status quo*, which they promote, do not recommend deterrence as the means of obtaining British safety in Europe in the indefinite future. The alternative to indefinite deterrence is some scheme of international security. The gradual establishment of such a system is not without dangers, but they are no greater than those existing in the present pursuit of defence, and the creative potential of a security system is ultimately far greater. It is therefore to be preferred morally, and for the chance it offers to a second-class power like Britain to play a positive role in the strategic-political future of Europe.

CONCLUSION

A number of future strategic courses open to Britain have been examined in this chapter. Of these, three are particularly noteworthy.

1. British governments may continue to give absolute priority to defence and to the solidarity of Nato. In effect this means increasing the transnational impact of Nato on herself, and it implies a continued stress on the leadership of the United States and on the strategic initiative of the existing first-rank powers.
2. British governments may join in an effort to increase the strategic independence of Western Europe by joining in the creation of a European nuclear capability. This politically formidable project would undermine the first course: or it might be the consequence of the collapse of the first course.
3. British governments may work towards the establishment of a security organisation in Europe to which national military forces would be committed. This course would be the negation of the second alternative, but, in its earlier phases, need have relatively little effect on the first course.

The essence of traditional sovereignty lies in the control of the state over its own means of going to war. Each of these three principal alternatives fundamentally abridges this power.

D

5 The economic predicament

An earlier chapter distinguished two broad images of the international economy of the Western industrialised countries: the image of an arena in which related sovereign states of varying autonomy exercise power and influence over one another in the pursuit of their national interests; and, second, a system of highly interdependent components in which the concepts of national sovereignty and autonomy are anachronisms standing in the way of rational international order. These simple and starkly contrasting images are partly devices to clarify some of the issues of economic foreign policy. The first does not exclude international agreement and cooperation to secure national economic benefits and to maintain international economic relations at a mutually advantageous level. And the second does not propose that national governments be abolished, merely that they should be reduced in their economic authority to a status analogous to that of the constituent provinces in an enlightened federation. It is unlikely that reality will approximate closely to either of these images, but by their economic foreign policies governments will determine whether international relations will veer to one pole or the other. This chapter proceeds by first examining the possible situation of Britain in relation to these two contrasting images of the nature of the international economy, and, secondly, by examing the situation of the European Community as a whole in the same way.

BRITAIN ON HER OWN

Given that the international economy approximates to an arena of power struggle between states, it follows that Britain must use sovereignty both to increase its national autonomy and power and to realise its national economic goals. Britain should free domestic policies of the arduous constraints formerly imposed by payments deficits in the context of relatively fixed exchange rates by an indefinite commitment to the free movement of sterling exchange rates, and by the imposition of taxes and quantitative controls on imports whenever these seem necessary for balanced trade. The disturbing transnational effects of large speculative movements of capital could be alleviated in a number of traditional ways. Notable among these is the mutually supporting activities of central banks in shifting monetary reserves among themselves if conditions so require, which has been an established international device resting on mutual interests in the prevention of violent fluctuations on the international exchanges. The collapse of sterling is in no state's interests because sterling remains an international reserve asset of some importance. Because this is so, it might be argued, power is conferred on Britain to extract self-interested support from abroad as required. Transnational capital movements could also be tackled by direct control and taxation with a view to increasing the autonomy of British governments in their pursuit of internal goals requiring strict control of internal rates of interest and money supply. In the same style, foreign direct investment in Britain through multinational companies could be limited by sovereignty in the cause of increasing national autonomy. Ordinary legal weapons are sufficient to the control of foreign expansion and takeover in the British economy. Lagging domestic investment could also be tackled directly: British capital resources could be husbanded by taxes and outright legal prohibitions on capital exports. The problems of international liquidity and reserve assets could be tackled along established lines on the basis of orthodox international negotiation: international liquidity in terms of dollars, sterling and other currencies, with the minor addition of SDRs, is anyway likely to remain adequate. There need be no necessary connection between growth in international trade and growth of international reserves provided that balance of payments adjustments can be made quickly by the sovereign methods indicated. Large international reserves are required to deal with large imbalances, but if there are no large imbalances there need be no large reserves. The matter of Britain's tendency to disequilibrium on capital account might be dealt with by rigorously reducing governmental expenditure abroad and by direct controls on private foreign investment. By such means, then, British foreign economic policy could be placed completely at the disposal of the pursuit of domestic economic goals. Milieu goals, analogous to security in the strategic sense employed earlier, would be entirely secondary.

The disadvantages of this kind of foreign policy might be experienced at three levels: the actual frustration of domestic economic policies, the dislocation of the international economic milieu to a degree harmful to Britain, and the political consequences of taking so sovereign an approach.

Britain remains a country heavily involved in international trade, and deficient, it may reasonably be argued, in domestic investment. The unilateral imposition of direct controls on imports exposes Britain to retaliation which could be more harmful than any benefits which might accrue, since Britain is relatively more dependent on imports than most of her trading partners are upon her exports. Stringent direct control on British overseas investment does not necessarily increase domestic investment, particularly if markets at home and abroad seem to be contracting. Direct restriction of the activities of foreign-owned multinational companies exposes Britain to retaliation by the companies themselves and by foreign governments on British-based multinational companies abroad. And a decline in foreign investment in Britain is directly harmful in that it removes 'imported' competitiveness from British industry and thus worsens Britain's trading position. There can be no assumption of an increase of domestic investment effort to compensate for it. Harshly sovereign control of foreign assets lodged in Britain is unlikely to destroy the transnational money market but merely drive it away from Britain. This market is a source of working capital and it brings financial business to this country. It also facilitates foreign currency borrowings by public bodies in Britain, which may be encouraged by governments anxious to cover balance of payments deficits.

It may be contended, then, that the total assertion of economic sovereignty could be directly harmful to the pursuit of domestic goals, because Britain's political sovereignty is not to be equated with economic autonomy. British sovereignty cannot be exercised from an established basis of autonomy. Bringing autonomy and sovereignty into balance means, in the present context, increasing autonomy; but increasing autonomy could be directly harmful to domestic economic policy.

Effects in terms of the economic milieu could be no less serious. A total and catching dedication to indefinitely fluctuating exchange rates could introduce a very high element of risk and uncertainty into the financing of world trade. If this caused an overall decline in international trade Britain might suffer more than most, because of her relatively great involvement in trade and because of the traditionally uncompetitive nature of sectors of British industry. Balance of payments equilibrium maintained by unrestrained exchange rate fluctuation does not dissolve problems of equitable adjustment if surplus countries take to maintaining stable exchange rates: as a deficit country in these circumstances Britain would be unable to bring pressure to bear on surplus countries to revalue their currencies since she has little in the way of economic power to deploy. And by contributing to an international milieu in which aid to underdeveloped countries would be a strictly national, not a multinational activity, Britain would reduce her own impact on the problem of economic backwardness, since what Britain alone could accomplish would be severely limited by domestic resources and domestic pressures.

At the political level, an assertion of economic sovereignty by British governments could have a number of serious consequences both for Britain and the international milieu. Most obviously, it would have disruptive effect on the EEC. Direct controls on trade would be an infringement of Community obligations. And a permanently individual approach to exchange rate problems would not merely complicate common European internal policies, but fundamentally contradict the Community programme to establish a common currency. It is unlikely that Britain could destroy EEC in this way, but she might very well exclude herself from it. Such an exclusion would not merely disrupt the growing element of British trade with Europe, it would also reduce the influence of British governments on European governments in all spheres, economic and otherwise. British rejection of the Community would additionally place Europeans in a position, psychologically and otherwise, to discriminate against Britain. Reliance on mutual aid between central banks might be misplaced in these circumstances. The international role of sterling is not essential to European prosperity, and would become even less so were the Europeans to go ahead with their plans for a common currency. The Community is not Britain's only international economic obligation. A disruptive impact on the GATT and on attempts to find a more creative role for the IMF would reduce the coherence of Western society generally and further hamper efforts to utilise these bodies to increase world trade generally and to confer upon disadvantaged countries enlightened treatment in the international economy. Harming goals such as these would confer no long-run benefit on Britain.

A British dedication to the indefinite maintenance of existing international reserve assets would seem to mean the permanent acceptance of the dominance of the dollar in international monetary relations. In the past this has sometimes been equated with a cavalier attitude on the part of the United States towards external economic and political influences, so this kind of policy on the part of Britain could be interpreted as a commitment to the economic hegemony of the United States, and this would be pointless unless accompanied by an equal commitment to American strategic dominance. So in the exercise of sovereignty, British governments could be submitting themselves to a vassal status in relation to the United States. Such an extreme Anglo-Saxon policy would certainly create enemies in Europe, and, in view of the reluctance of American governments to allow foreigners to participate in the machinery of American foreign policy, economic and otherwise, is hardly likely to increase the impact of British governments on world events generally.

If the absolute priority of domestic economic goals, and the pursuit of domestic economic autonomy, required reductions in British governmental expenditure overseas, then British military activities outside Europe would finally come to an end. And Britain might even feel impelled to liquidate her military presence in Nato. Reducing British influence abroad is a curious consequence of the assertion of sovereignty. Taking Britain out of the European strategic arena means taking Britain out of the European search for defence and for security. It would also mean cutting off a channel of influence on American strategic policies.

BRITAIN SUBMERGED

The establishment of national autonomy through the exercise of national sovereignty has as its opposite the pursuit of international integration through the abandonment of national sovereignty. This is the image of the Western economy as a single interdependent whole, for which it should be the task of statesmen to fashion appropriate authoritative institutions. This is an image of a world environment in which goods, capital, labour and skill would move freely. Multi-national businesses would operate within the setting of harmonised international regulations relating to taxation and monopolies. Problems of exchange rate fluctuations would be abolished by the creation of a single currency, regulated by an authoritative international institution capable of creating liquidity and of mopping it up as economic needs require.

The problems of realising such an environment are formidable. A common currency does not abolish the balance of payments problem because territories which import more than they export are still likely to suffer a decline in investment and employment. But when a common currency exists these intensely human problems cannot be tackled by an exchange rate change designed to restore competitiveness. Instead, more direct policies must be undertaken, in the absence of swift large-scale emigration from hard-hit areas. These regional policies take familiar forms such as investment grants, employment premiums, public works, and the like, whose purpose is usually the restoration of competitiveness by the use of discriminatory public aid. In other words, the creation of a common international currency, if it is to carry any kind of political conviction, must be associated with coordinated, internationally sanctioned economic policies relating to employment, economic growth, and the maintenance of a uniform rate of inflation (or, even more remotely, no inflation at all) over the area covered by the common currency. So a common currency must be associated with completely authoritative common political institutions, because policies of these kinds are part of the intimate fabric of politics itself.

The creation of such a milieu is related to three broad possibilities: first, to the use of an existing national currency, the dollar, which already has a political authority of a kind, the United States government; second, to the use of an existing international currency, perhaps the eurodollar, and the creation of a new international authority for it; third, to the creation of an entirely new international currency and a new authority, and here the most obvious candidate is a refurbished IMF.

Hitherto the United States government has not shown itself markedly open to overseas economic influence and the possibility of transforming it into some kind of international government raises constitutional difficulties of an impossibly formidable kind. In relation to the second possibility, the eurodollar is not so much a currency as an international market in a variety of currencies, and its chief characteristic is its fluidity, its capacity to evade tight regulation. Thirdly, the elevation of the IMF, with its SDRs, to the status of authoritative form of international economic government would be a daunting task, analogous to the creation of a world government capable of enforcing a world security system. The IMF, of course, includes representatives of governments outside the Western industrialised circle. It is a slow-moving body whose members are fully occupied in bringing about relatively small changes, such as the creation of SDRs in the first place and the development of flexible practices in their allocation. The IMF has some resources, it imposes some obligations on borrowers, but it is not a government in any political sense. In the past its rules have been more than honoured in the breach by almost all the governments formally bound by them.

The aim of creating a fully integrated international economy would involve Britain either in accepting and promoting American hegemony, or in abandoning instruments of economic regulation to institutions which would be incapable of operating policies to deal directly with underlying economic problems. Neither course has much practical merit.

THE EEC AND SOVEREIGNTY

The next set of possibilities draws a little nearer the realm of practice. This is the creation of a European Community with economic autonomy, capable of exercising a new sovereignty in an effective manner in the pursuit of its own interests. The promise of a new sovereignty and a matching economic autonomy can be detected in the Treaty of Rome and in the programmes which have been indistinctly attached to it. The essential condition of a new political sovereignty would be met if a European executive were linked to a legitimate, directly elected European Parliament. Economic autonomy would be the product of a high level of intra-European economic activity, a common currency, and coherent governmental instruments of economic intervention and foreign action. Assuming for present purposes that these formidable conditions of sovereignty and autonomy could be achieved, and accepting the model of the international economy as an arena in which states exert power and influence over one another, to what purposes could the new state of Western Europe exert itself?

The first task, by definition, would be the reduction of foreign power over Europe. The principal national centre of this alien power is the United States, and its European manifestations these: first, the capacity for pressure conferred on the United States as the only guarantor of the dollars which comprise the bulk of European reserves; second, the means of direct control created by American direct investment in Western Europe in the shape of American-controlled multinational companies; third, the basic impediment to European autonomy created by the unstable swell of dollars in the international market which undermines the pursuit of independent European monetary policies. An effective European government, a strong European currency, a common European capital market and a single European central bank would place invincible weapons in the hands of Europeans with which they could counter these effects. Europe could cease to bolster the United States by mopping up surplus dollars as required, the holders of foreign currencies in Europe could be penalised by taxes and other direct controls, dollar investment in Europe could be curtailed by discriminatory measures, American businesses in Europe could be taken over by Europeans and their American owners compensated from the stock of officially held dollars in Europe, and so on. The conditions of this programme might even confer direct benefits on Britain by the removal of the burden of overseas sterling balances, which would be converted into European currency (though Britain would presumably pay a small rate of interest on liabilities assumed by Europe in this way). It might even prove possible for sterling itself to form the basis of the European currency. In these ways, then, Europeans could use economic strength to reduce the power of the United States and increase the power of Western Europe. Trade policy could be used to extend European influence in areas of vital strategic and economic importance to Europeans by an extension of the practice of making preferential trading agreements with third countries, particularly in the Mediterranean area. By means such as these European strength could be harnessed to provide the substance of a large international region in which European authorities could act out the role of a superpower.

As a prospective programme the creation and use of a European sovereignty raises difficulties and disadvantages which may be conveniently surveyed in the context, first, of intra-European relations, and, second, in terms of relations between Europe and the rest of the world.

Sovereignty has been used here to denote the political power to act; autonomy has been used to denote the extent to which given conditions confer scope within which the actions of the sovereign may be effective. Thus, for example, a British government, using British sovereignty, could erect a very high tariff wall around the United Kingdom: but British autonomy is of such a nature that it is difficult to imagine circumstances, other than the collapse of the international economy, in which such an action would have other than extremely harmful consequences for Britain. Sovereignty and autonomy are related but they are not identical. It is conceivable that the European Community could attain a relatively high measure of autonomy, yet fail to develop an effective sovereignty. A prominent feature of the political life of the Community hitherto has been its slow and involved processes of making decisions, and its rigidity in changing circumstances. If this bureaucratic-diplomatic style continues unabridged in the future, the image of Europe acting out the role of an assertive sovereign is not one which carries much conviction. The political obstacles to the creation of a single, effective European political authority (and if it were created problems of British economic foreign policy would disappear in the problems of Community foreign policy) are formidable and will be touched on at a later stage; sufficient to point out now that such an objective requires the transformation of European politics into a fairly coherent kind of domestic politics. The implications of such a transformation in terms of the integration of political parties, of modes of representation, conventions of political conduct, and of popular attitudes to political authority are more than intractable.

The goal of a common currency, though it has become a recognised part of the European programme, is fraught with intense political difficulties. As indicated in an earlier context, the freezing of exchange rates in perpetuity, which is the final manifestation of a common currency, removes from national governments an important tool in the pursuit of domestic policy objectives such as full employment and the restoration of international competitiveness in conditions of domestic inflation. Thus progress towards a European currency must be matched, and probably preceded, by the development of common European policies towards such matters as inflation and regional economic adjustment. The relentless narrowing of mutual exchange rate oscillations, a necessary element in the approach to a common currency, could create balance of payments difficulties for less competitive European countries. Deficits run up in this cause would have to be balanced by direct assistance from surplus countries, but these might be reluctant to subsidise others or might be inclined to use their resources to strike unwelcome political bargains.

However, supposing economic sovereignty and economic autonomy to be in prospect, would their use in the way imagined in this scenario be conducive to British values or British interests? This essay began by noting the discontinuities observable in the present international environment; an assertively sovereign Europe would add further discontinuities to those already existing. In this way it might strike a blow at those institutions which attempt to bridge world discontinuities. The further division of the world is hardly a prospect congenial to a liberal vision of increasing international interdependence and order. But the central difficulty of these possibilities of European sovereignty and autonomy, from an orthodox British viewpoint, lies in their effects on relations between the United States and Europe. Policies such as active discrimination against American trade and investment, and attacks on the American currency, would almost certainly instigate retaliatory moves in the United States. This kind of trans-Atlantic battle would harm the network of world trade, in which both Britain and Western Europe are more heavily involved than the United States, and would be directly disastrous to British and European multi-national businesses deeply committed in the United States and to holders of portfolio investments there. More important than effects of these kinds could be the harm caused to the Atlantic defence community. A breakdown of economic relations would spill over into this strategic defence system, which is presently squarely founded on American military strength. A previous chapter indicated some of the possible consequences of a removal of the American strategic guarantee to Europe. It would almost certainly press Western Europeans to embark on the task of acquiring a first-class military capability of their own. A programme of economic autonomy and sovereignty would thus press Western Europe towards a programme of nuclear autonomy and sovereignty. The internal difficulties in the European Community of such a task have already been indicated. Externally, the addition of another first-class military power to the international arena would hardly add to the total of international safety, and could add little but greater rigidity to the European *status quo*. The spectacle of a new first-rank state on her western borders would not be one to encourage a relaxation of the Soviet hold on Eastern Europe, rather the reverse. A fresh contender in the nuclear race would make the international regulation of armaments and the creation of an international security system more difficult than they already are. More nuclear strength does not mean more safety.

The emphasis on the European–American strategic connection, which has been at the core of postwar British foreign policy, loses none of its force simply because the form of British economic policy is required to adapt itself to closer Western European relations.

THE COMMUNITY, INTERDEPENDENCE AND STATES

So far this chapter has considered extreme policies. It concludes by considering the possibilities of a liberal programme in a world conceived to lie somewhere between the extremes of interdependence and conflicting national sovereignties. The international economy is not an ogre; nor is it an unalloyed benefit to its members if it is left unattended by international authorities. The fundamental challenge of this milieu is that of establishing an order which can reconcile the facts of inter-dependence and of the existence of unequal states with governments politically absorbed in the pursuit of domestic economic goals.

This problem of order is most vividly demonstrated in the international monetary system, where interdependence in a milieu in which authority is concentrated in states produces intense international stresses. In 1970, for example, an American government, concerned to stimulate the American economy, took measures to lower domestic interest rates: in consequence, large quantities of dollars moved overseas in search of higher rates of return, thereby worsening American balance of payments deficits and causing German authorities, then maintaining relatively 'tight' internal monetary policies, to acquire large quantities of immigrant American currency to maintain stable exchange rates. The German and American governments collaborated, the German government contributing rather more than the American, to deal with the problem and the Bundesbank repeatedly reduced its discount rate, thus negating domestic policies of tight money and high interest rates. Despite these efforts, general agitation about the condition of the dollar stimulated continued large-scale movements into Germany and on 5 May 1971 the Bundesbank was forced to close the German foreign exchange market. The immediate outcome of this particular crisis was that, in the absence of further action on the part of an American Administration on the approach to the 1972 presidential elections, the German authorities allowed the mark to float upwards. This decision disrupted the price parities of the EEC common agricultural policy and negated a Community decision to reduce currency fluctuation margins in the cause of monetary union. The Community itself was unable to produce joint policies towards the overvaluation of the dollar, and towards the gigantic size and flexibility of the eurodollar market, such as might have relieved Germany of the necessity to act unilaterally. Similarly, unilateral floating, of course, contradicted IMF principles as they then were; at the same time the IMF's puny control and disposition of international credit was entirely inadequate to the scale of the movements taking place in the Western international economy.

This crisis was simply an episode in a larger, longer and continuing disturbance, which the actions of the German government did not resolve. It is mentioned here only for illustrative purposes. It revealed an American government uninterested in taking close responsibility for the international movements of its currency. The two outstanding transnational institutions of the Western economy, the IMF and the EEC, were relatively powerless to handle its problems. The actions which individual governments (the German government in this very limited example) felt themselves obliged to take ran contrary to specific international institutional obligations and, even more significantly, to existing internal policies. No effective international or national pressure was brought to bear upon the United States. Overall, this episode, and the longer crisis of which it was a part, illustrated the capacity of the Western economy to distract and obsess its members to the partial exclusion of concern for the problems of the poorer parts of the world.

Assuming that Britain, always absorbed in the pursuit of her own domestic economic goals, is externally concerned, first, for the maintenance of the Atlantic defence system; second, for realising mutual interests with her neighbours and partners in EEC; third, for achieving political and economic order among all the principal states of the Western international economy; and, fourth, for the mobilisation of the resources of this economy for the benefit of poorer peoples; then some familiar programmes for British economic foreign policy may be quickly outlined.

European economic integration, not necessarily union, is stressed. This local objective may be held desirable because it would create conditions in which European authorities could effectively coordinate their efforts to control financial markets which threaten their stability. It might offer the chance of insulating Europe from disturbance by the 'slop' of dollars between individual countries, those consequences, hitherto, have been to throw European currencies into disarray. It could also confer on European authorities economic and monetary strength from which to negotiate effectively with governments of the United States, thus creating a more equitable political balance within the international economy as a whole. More selfishly, from a British viewpoint, it might offer an eventual opportunity to liquidate the reserve role of sterling. Similarly, European unity in the face of scarce energy resources might help to keep down the international price of oil, while allowing Britain to import capital to develop her indigenous fuel supplies for the benefit of herself and her neighbours.

An equally familiar programme urges the desirability of finding some means for converting dollar balances held by monetary authorities into international assets, internationally regulated. These assets, and SDRs clearly qualify for this role, would consequently become a major source of international liquidity and a major reserve asset of central banks. This goal could be achieved if official holders of dollars were given the opportunity to convert these American liabilities into SDRs, on which the United States would then pay a rate of interest. The supersession in this style of the dollar by the SDR would necessarily be accompanied by the elevation of the IMF into a more powerful organisation, exercising control over the supply of a major international currency. An IMF promoted to this role might be encouraged by British governments and their European partners to exercise its powers creatively, by, for example, placing at the disposal of less developed countries credits sufficient for them to sustain sizeable balance of payments deficits. Meanwhile the European Community would itself play an openhanded role in dealing with the trade and investment problems of the Third World. Additionally, the Community might be led to foreswear restrictive attitudes to trade, put its weight behind the GATT, and relieve the United States of worries about the creation of an exclusive trading bloc centred on Western Europe. The Community should also seek means of drawing the Eastern European countries into the network of Western European economic relations.

There are many variants of programmes such as these, and many permutations among them. Their most striking common feature is the central place of tansnational organisations in them. Transnational organisation is seen as a means of increasing British influence on Britain's neighbours in Europe. British influence on the United States is seen to be mediated and perhaps strengthened by transnational organisations in Europe and in the Western economy at large. Britain is shown to be intimately concerned about relations between organisations, between the EEC and the GATT and the IMF in the present examples. The problems of the Third World are seen in terms of increasing the effectiveness of organisations. More striking still, the pursuit of specific national goals (a large market and sources of much-needed capital for purposes of domestic economic expansion, release from the bondage of the international role of sterling, greater autonomy in the face of international monetary disorders) is also perceived to require active British participation in transnational organisations which British governments cannot hope to dominate.

The central role of transnational intergovernmental organisations in the future of British economic foreign policy creates four sorts of problems. First, there is the paradox of operating a national foreign policy whose successful outcome requires a transformation of national foreign policy. To take the position that it is more possible to influence the policies of other governments through transnational organisations than through traditional interstate diplomacy is to accept two premises: that one will be open to the reciprocal influence of other governments in matters of internal political and economic delicacy; and that one believes that it is both possible and desirable to build transnational organisations with their own standing as international actors. Yet, as a matter of practical government conduct, the approach to transnational organisation starts from the standpoint of sovereignty, which is here taken to mean the political capability to ignore transnational organisations. The existence of this capability clearly undermines the potential standing of these organisations as international actors. Governments are reluctant to surrender control of the instruments with which they may hope to pursue domestic objectives. Any transnational scheme which seeks to control exchange rates will be treated with reserve by British governments anxious to preserve exchange rate flexibility as an instrument with which to maintain domestic economic growth. Though a British government has indicated acceptance of the need for European monetary coordination, the immediately practical matter of linking sterling exchange rates more closely with those of the currencies of her Community partners has been approached with extreme caution. The immediate practical response of the British government to the oil crisis of 1973 was not to stress European unity but to ride British sovereignty in pursuit of a primarily national solution.

Second, there are the associated questions relating to the competence, actual and potential, of intergovernmental transnational organisations. The IMF was conspicuous among our specimen programmes of British economic foreign policy. But even modest hopes for the future of this organisation cannot ignore its past weaknesses. Its foundation principle of stable exchange rates has been universally ignored. Its first allocations of SDRs were made on the most unenterprising of sharing principles: to each according to the size of his existing quota with the Fund, or, more bluntly, to each according to his national power. The evolution of any more bold principle is likely to be a slow and cautious process, particularly in view of the horror which Western governments have of adding to the inflationary pressures they already endure. The IMF operates under a weighted voting system which confers on wealthy countries, particularly the United States, a veto over Fund actions. The official servants of the Fund are also the servants of the members of the Fund and must attempt to make themselves agreeable to the more powerful among them. For traditional political reasons such as these, programmes which place the IMF at the authoritative centre of the Western monetary system can easily drift into unrealism. In attempting to avoid this kind of drift, this essay has treated the prospect of complete monetary union in the European Community with circumspection. It is probably true that a common European currency would confer great international power on European authorities. But if this goal is removed to the remote future, the Community must struggle along with intermediate measures of monetary coordination. Such measures tend to be complicated, and, by definition, they can be ignored. Though they may add to the organisational apparatus of Europe, it is therefore questionable whether they can in any way add to the international strength of European governments. If, because of their constant concern with the intermediate, transnational organisations can acquire no real power, then it may seem to follow that the prospect of their providing channels whereby lesser governments, such as those of Britain, could exercise an enhanced influence on their milieu may be chimerical. Britain, however, has little alternative but to pursue this goal, whether it be real or illusory.

Third, there are the problems of complementarity in the transnational milieu. Our specimen British foreign policy programmes were built on the assumption that different transnational organisations, the IMF and the EEC most prominently, can operate in a complementary fashion. This need not be so, if only because the more effective one of these organisations becomes the less need is there for the other: the more effective the IMF, the less compelling is the case for the European governments to draw together for monetary defence; the stronger the EEC, the fewer the international hazards facing European governments and the less pressing is their need for effective transnational organisations in the extra-European setting. There is a further problem of complementarity which is intrinsic to the penetration of states. This is the problem of the complementarity of transnational intergovernmental organisations and government and politics within national systems. Complementarity between the structures of EEC and the values of British democracy is questionable, and will be taken up at a later stage.

Fourth, there is the fundamental problem as to whether transnational organisations are always likely to serve basic British policy objectives. This problem presents itself at two levels. At the first level, it cannot be assumed that selfish British concerns with increased wealth are necessarily served by these organisations. The possibility that EEC might develop into a restrictive bloc, dislocative of world trade as a whole, is one which must raise doubts on this score, as does EEC's propensity to impose balance of payments costs on Britain. At the second level, it is by no means assured that Britain's milieu goals are served by transnational economic organisations. Ultimately, it may be argued, economic foreign policy has to be assessed in its impact on the United States and on the defence system, vital to British safety, of which this power is the keystone. The specimen programmes with which we began emphasised the search by European second-rankers for a more equitable distribution of power in the Western economic system through transnational organisations. Thus the European Community could effectively measure its strength beside that of the United States; additionally, or alternatively, wider organisations such as the IMF could be made more effective and thus open the economic milieu to greater regulatory participation by lesser powers. But these goals can be interpreted as attacks on the power and influence of the United States. If they were perceived in this way, and if they were pressed in the face of this perception, the disruptive consequences of American reaction could seriously undermine the Atlantic defence system. As we have seen, the existing international economic system can be regarded as one which both expresses and sustains the power of the United States. If this is so, it follows that fundamental changes in the organisation of this system could diminish American power, and this American governments are likely to resist.

CONCLUSION

The economic actions of governments are also political actions. The economic and political circumstances of Britain have led her govern ments to stress the role of intergovernmental transnational or- ganisations in foreign economic policy. The more effective these organisations become, the greater is the transformation of British foreign policy. The political problems of economic and governmental trans-nationalism are formidable. Four sets of these problems are particularly noteworthy: first, the stresses of the integrative process in Europe; second, the problems created by the uncertain future of American attitudes to transnational intergovernmental organisations; third, the problems of achieving complementarity between transnational organisations, and between transnational organisations and national governments; fourth, the problems created by the linkages between the transnational Western defence system and the economic system. There are few likely outcomes, and no desirable ones, of these problems which could release Britain from absorption in transnational economic relations and transnational organisations. The optimum solution for British governments is the harmonisation of transnationalism in Europe with transnationalism in the Western economy, and this must be linked with a continuing nervous regard for the maintenance of American–European partnership.

6 The institutional predicament

CHANGE

British foreign policy can be analysed in terms of an institutional frame of reference which dictates that sovereign states are the units of all internationally significant action, that states relate to one another through the medium of diplomacy, that diplomacy is the institutional means whereby states deploy their sovereign strength to secure their interests. Given these parameters, the changes affecting modern British foreign policy may be simply tabulated.

1. British strength has declined relatively to the point at which Britain is placed among the second-class states. Her sovereign bargaining strength is thus so reduced that it can only be expected to be used with effect at a local level. The locality in question is Britain's immediate geographical surroundings in Western Europe.
2. In Western Europe Britain is in no way the superior of at least two other states, France and the German Federal Republic.
3. Two extraregional, first-class states are engaged in Europe. Neither Britain nor the other European second-rank states can mount a convincing deterrent to the Soviet Union. Nor can Britain exercise much direct power over the United States. The power she has in relation to the United States is conferred on her by that state's commitment to the *status quo* in Europe. A diminution of that commitment would also reduce British power in relation to the United States.
4. The United States and the Soviet Union occupy the highest stratum of the hierarchy of states, and their diplomatic relationship is a direct one which could become exclusive. Their conflict relationship is most clearly expressed in the European theatre: but, in nuclear terms particularly, their interests draw them towards cooperative diplomatic enterprises.

5. In economic terms, Britain offers a small internal market to its producers. Britain has compensated for this, and for the decline of the Commonwealth-sterling bloc, by entering the EEC customs union.
6. Britain remains heavily involved in trade and monetary relations outside the new European customs union. These relations are particularly concentrated in the circle of advanced capitalist countries. In this network of relations the United States is the most powerful single state; and the United States exerts this power to secure its own interests.

Given these 'facts' of the British predicament, Britain can either accept the role of vassal of the United States, hoping that United States interests will remain of such a nature as to confer some influence on her, or she can attempt to increase her power and thus act directly on the international environment to secure her own interests. In the latter case she must, by definition, either attempt to play on the conflict relationship of the first-rank powers or align herself with comparable states in Western Europe. If the first of these courses is ruled out by its dangers and by the fact that the first-rankers have a strong mutual interest in stability and in preventing irresponsible outside intrusion into their relationship, then alignment in Western Europe is the only course open to Britain. The programme of such an alignment is suggested by the kinds of motivations behind its formation. By deploying their strength jointly Britain and the other Western European second-rank states should discourage the United States from entering into arrangements with the Soviet Union which might be harmful to their interests. Similarly, in the economic field they should exert themselves to prevent the development of American hegemony in the international economy. Should these objectives prove unattainable, the Western European allies should mobilise their strength to secure their own independent defence, and, second, should build up their economic autonomy to secure their economic wellbeing from the harmful effects of the economic foreign policies of other powers.

This kind of programme is attended by a number of internal inconsistencies. The initial force of joint Western European policies is to be directed, quite logically, against the power most heavily involved and influential in Western European affairs, that is the United States. But the United States is currently the ally of the Western European states. If the effect of the Western European alliance is to undermine the Atlantic alliance, it follows that the Western European alliance should be able and willing to conduct its own relations with the Soviet Union and other external powers without dependence on the strength or agency of the United States. But the nature of the institutions of international relations are such that the mutually aligned defence policies of the Western European states cannot deploy a military strength equivalent to that of one of the first-rank powers. States are indissoluble and the aligned forces of second-rankers cannot equal the single force of one first-ranker. This is as true of economic policy as of defence policy. Placing Western Europe in the first rank economically presupposes the creation of a first-rank economic strength in Western Europe: but this requires an economic union with a common currency. But the creation of a common currency means the abandonment by states of their sovereign authority, and this, by definition, is impossible. Additionally, decades must pass before Western Europe as a whole develops its own sources of energy on a first-rank scale. The sharing of British oil resources would reduce British strength without markedly increasing that of the Community.

In this kind of way, traditional parameters push one to a conclusion which lies outside those parameters, the creation of a new Western European state. Accepting this to be impossible, it follows that Britain should continue to move diplomatically, along pragmatic lines as different issues require, to maintain some semblance of coherence in the foreign policies of the principal Western states. It also follows, given that diplomacy is the deployment of the strength and sovereignty of the state, that ultimately the United States must exert more influence on Britain than Britain can hope to exert on the United States, and that ultimately the United States must also exert more influence on Britain than any Western European state or group of states. Given that the traditional frame of reference rules out the possibility of fundamental change, though, in a sense, recommending it, British foreign policy is explicable entirely in terms of declining strength, which, in the future as in the past, will lead Britain to place her diplomatic alignment with the United States at the core of her foreign policy; and this priority must prompt a reserved approach to European alignment.

TRANSFORMATION

Let us now abandon the frame of reference which yields conclusions and predictions of this kind, and assume that global relations comprise a complex field of pressures and communications to which no clear parameters (the sovereign state, power diplomacy, national interest) can be applied. The field as such does not set limits to structural transformations. In this field, authority, never a constant quality, is conferred on governments principally, though not exclusively, by national politics. Problems assail governments, and demands are made on them, in the context of the global field. Internal political demands may be stimulated by external influences. Though authority may be conferred principally by national politics, its expenditure in efforts to govern are therefore not restricted by national boundaries. The concerns of governments are twofold: first, to render governable the field of stresses within which they exist; and, second, to use this governability to achieve specific ends. These two concerns are closely related in the sense that governability depends on the existence of agreements, traditions, conventions and theories relating to what governments can and should do. In the context of stable domestic politics, governability is a quality which is generally conferred on governments from the outset of their endeavours; though even for British governments a goodly share of government effort must be expended on the maintenance or extension of internal governability. The wider the field of operations of governments, the more laboriously must they be engaged in establishing a measure of governability rather than in governing. This is a distinction of degree, not of kind, between the international and national settings of government.

Given these notions of international relations, the principal transnational changes affecting British politics and government may be simply tabulated.

1. The search for the governability of purely destructive international potential through policies of defence and power balance has led to the creation of transnational intergovernmental organisations (principally Nato) which involve British governments in the attempt to regulate the strategies and dispositions of military forces which are not British and which also expose British forces to reciprocal foreign influences.

2. In the nuclear age, the governability of destructive forces through defence cannot be expected to provide a high degree of safety, since defence concentrates transnational regulation in only a limited sector of the strategic system. The pursuit of safety through security (through, that is, the establishment of governability in the system as a whole) must, for a time, coexist with defence policies. The

achievement of any measure of governability through security must mean increasing the number of national authorities involved in the regulation of some military establishments. Slight beginnings of an approach to security may be detected at the highest level of potential destructiveness in the closer relations of Soviet and American governments in matters relating to the control of strategic weapons.

3. There has been a massive increase in the economic demands made upon British governments. Greater authority for intervention in economic affairs has also been conferred on British governments. But the scope of this additional authority does not in itself provide the basis of authoritative actions which can match the scale of demands which are made upon governments. The British economy is open to large transnational forces in the shape of disturbances to world trade, movements of capital, and suchlike. In the international economy with which Britain is so closely linked, British governments do not rank as prominent authorities. This international economy substantially rests on the postwar political order centred on the United States. This order has been expressed in the creation of a number of transnational intergovernmental organisations, notably the IMF and the GATT. This kind of transnational search for governability is impeded by two general problems: first, by the problem of striking a balance between the requirements of transnational order and the retention by national governments of their control and use of policy instruments; second, by the problem of the propensity of governments to conduct their economic foreign policies by extra-organisational methods.

4. An attempt by a British government to achieve its economic objectives through the use of sovereignty and the cultivation of autonomy is unlikely to be successful. While Britain is deeply involved in the transnational Western economy the problem of order and governability in this wider setting will be a vital one for British governments. 'Defence' from the pressures and problems of the wider economic setting might be sought through the creation of a relatively autonomous sovereignty in the European Community. This response to transnationalism, which is traditional in its assumption that a state can only be changed by being replaced by another state, has two fundamental drawbacks: first, it demands the almost total abandonment of instruments of economic control and intervention by the national governments concerned, which is not likely

to be forthcoming; second, it creates a new discontinuity within the Western international economy, pushing it further towards the model of an arena of power conflict and further qualifying its prospects of order and governability. The latter outcome has important dislocative implications for the international strategic system.

5. The political importance of international economic action has increased and shows no sign of diminishing. This is so for three fundamental reasons: first, massive decisions of peace and war appear to have been isolated in a system dominated by the two first-rank governments where they seem to have been stabilised by a common interest in avoiding nuclear war; second, direct military intervention abroad has become uncongenial to most Western powers, and this removes the element of direct military strength from a large number of foreign policy questions, even those relating to the maintenance of vital supplies of oil; third, the economic demands on British governments are mirrored, and often magnified, in most other countries. Though economic policy has increased in importance, the greater the element of transnational organisation and order in the international economy, the less sense does it make to think in terms of national economic foreign policy. Thus, for example, British concerns in economic relations with poorer countries must be substantially expressed through the actions of the EEC, GATT, IMF, and the like. What Britain does in these circumstances is to participate in the formulation of the foreign policies of these bodies and of the transnational systems upon which they operate.

Given that international relations comprise a field to which no fixed institutional parameters apply, a number of intellectual difficulties created by concepts of the state, foreign policy, power, diplomacy and suchlike, disappear and it is possible to discuss wide future possibilities on the assumption of structural plasticity. Because of the open nature of the field of international relations, these possibilities cannot pretend to be definitive and they need not be mutually consistent.

1. The governability of destructive forces is not served by creating a new first-rank sovereignty in Western Europe. Overlooking the intractable internal resistances to such a project, it cannot provide much more safety through defence than existing Nato transnational arrangements. What it would add to safety by strength, it would detract from safety by adding a new source of instability to the

overall strategic system. Nor would it in any way ease the transition from safety through defence to safety through security.

2. The possibility of a measure of accord (including transnational elements) between the first-rank governments does not intrinsically constitute a threat to any other government seeking the governability of destructive forces through security. There are two general ways in which British governments could further this tendency to strategic governability: first, by avoiding actions which could destabilise the East–West strategic balance (by playing no part, for example, in the development or acquisition of weapons in Britain or Europe which could upset bargains struck between the first-rank governments relating to their respective holdings of nuclear missiles); second, by helping positively to establish a transnational security organisation in Europe which would contribute to the evolution of security arrangements between the first-rankers. Military transnationalism is an essential element in defence and security, and the primary institutional task is to adapt Nato to the service of both these policies. This is not an entirely safe course, because the pursuit of security could undermine defence for very little effective return in security.

3. In the same sort of way, transnational economic order is not furthered by the attempt to create an economic sovereignty in Western Europe. The development of intergovernmental transnationalism in Europe should therefore be linked with the similar enterprises in the wider international economic system. The primary institutional problem of governments is to harmonise transnational intergovernmental integration in Europe with integration in the wider environment. In the process, British governments should be concerned that joint economic policies, manifested through transnational organisations, should service overall political objectives, such as the maintenance of American–European intergovernmental and other linkages, the extension of economic ties with Eastern Europe, the provision to poorer countries of access to Western markets (including capital markets) on favourable terms, the involvement of the rich oil-producing countries in the networks of transnational economic order.

This kind of programme is almost wholly concerned with transnational intergovernmental organisations. It requires the adaptation of some existing organisations to purposes which may seem to be wider than those for which they were designed. Merging Nato, a transnational defence organisation, into the workings of a new transnational security organisation in Europe is a project bristling with political, military and organisational problems. Nato, among other things, is a repository of military secrets, but a security organisation must be the enemy of military secrets; Nato makes its arrangements with the prospects of attack from a specific quarter in mind, a security organisation containing members of both hostile camps cannot plan in terms of a specific prospective disturbance. In the same way, the Treaty of Rome is concerned with a programme of integration among its members. In the nature of its limited membership it could not have been expected to address itself to the task of transnational order in the Western international economy as a whole. In some senses, integration at the European and extra-European levels is a contradictory programme. If, for example, the IMF were to be developed in such a way as to resolve some of the more pressing problems of the transnational monetary system, Europeans, particularly the British, might feel less need for monetary integration in Europe to defend themselves from extra-European disturbances and to provide a joint power base from which to counter the strength of the United States. Conversely, a successful programme of integration in Europe, resulting in a high measure of autonomy, would make a larger programme of integration more difficult for two reasons; first, Europeans would feel less need for the larger programme, particularly if it seemed likely to undermine their newfound strength; second, the addition to the international economic system of a large new sovereign power, complicated and rigid in its internal processes and policies, is unlikely to further the political evolution of an appropriate transnational order in the wider setting.

A programme which is almost entirely concerned with organisation and process within and between transnational systems is one which cannot be contained within the categories of traditional foreign policy. An integrative process, involving a wide range of private and official groups and organisations, cannot be a controlled strategy of state diplomacy. If British economic and political forms of social life and British instruments of government, such as the army and the bureaucracy, are immersed in transnational relations, it follows that foreign policy as the exertion of the strength of the state to achieve power over other states in the service of the British national interest is an obsolete conception. Yet an approach which leads to this conclusion also leads one to a paradox: if one believes that one is confronted by an exceptionally complex field of national–international linkages to which the traditional language of foreign policy does not apply, how can it be possible to discuss British international policies at all?

CHANGE AND TRANSFORMATION

If state diplomacy is committed to the belief that there can be no fundamental transformation of foreign policy, then its actions must be structure-dominated; that is, it must perceive international issues wholly in terms of alignments and conflicts among states rather than as problems of order in transnational systems. Given the notion of sovereignty, state diplomacy also perceives international society as a congeries of bilateral relations between pairs of states; for if states are sovereign, groups of states must, by definition, be entirely unstable entities. Though states may align themselves from time to time in large groups, the constant underlying reality of diplomacy lies in flows of bilateral pressures and communications. From this viewpoint, the European Community exists as two sorts of particularly intense bilateral relations: those between Britain and each one of the other member states; and those between pairs of the other states as they impinge on British interests.

Traditional diplomacy must also be ideologically committed to the notion that the state, being the main actor in the international arena, possesses instruments of self-expression which it uses as its foreign policy requires. The sovereign state cannot share its means of expression in any deep sense. This attitude engenders profound reservations about, for example, the actual or prospective assignment of British forces to an array of transnational organisations concerned with defence and with security; similarly, the gradual merging of British officials into a transnational bureaucracy absorbed in, say, transnational economic problems, threatens to obscure the primary duty of civil servants to the state and thus to cripple the state's capabilities for international action.

Traditional diplomacy is structured to perform the task of representing a specific entity, the state, which is capable of expressing its sovereign will through a fairly coherent set of internal political institutions. If this internal political system breaks out of the boundaries of the state, if its citizens, representatives and bureaucrats become direct participants in transnational organisations and their assemblies, then an unwelcome element of confusion is created in diplomacy, which is no longer alone in its involvement in foreign politics. It can no longer claim to be the exclusive international representative of the sovereign because the sovereign itself, the internal political order, merges into its environment. Nor can diplomacy itself be encased within organisations, transnational or international. Sovereigns cannot be bound in the conduct of their essentially bilateral relations by procedures laid down for the conduct of relations among large groups of governments in transnational and international organisations. Though sovereigns may pay exact attention to the rules of diplomatic protocol, the premise of these rules is the inviolable integrity of sovereigns.

For reasons such as these, it may seem that this chapter has been delineating two views of the institutional nature of Britain's international predicament so distinctive as to yield mutually exclusive doctrines about the future nature and strategy of British foreign policy. The resolution of this conflict may be a matter requiring purely philosophical treatment. At the level of practice, there are five points of possible contact between these doctrines. First, transnational inter-governmental organisation may be seen as a use of the authority of governments to which the notion of sovereignty is not directly relevant. In transnational organisations governments are attempting to achieve greater effectiveness. These organisations are therefore not taking away power from governments but creating a transnational condition of order within which the power of specific governments to achieve goals considered politically desirable among their constituents is greater than it would be otherwise. This is a relationship of complementarity. Power is not taken away from governments and given to other kinds of institutions. Authority is deployed to maximise the effectiveness of governments.

Second, few statesmen or diplomatists actually take the view that all states are alike. In fact friendly states, states with similar values to those of the home state and with close practical and cultural ties with it, are markedly distinguished from truly alien states and possibly hostile states. Much of the transnational integrative process as it affects Britain creates, or is founded on, a network of relations among a group of friendly states, and is not therefore intrinsically repugnant to traditional foreign policy since it does not hazard British values or British safety.

Third, given the basic military fact of nuclear deterrence, state diplomacy must tend in Europe to be absorbed in the maintenance of the East–West *status quo*, if only because changing the *status quo* by the exertion of state strength could have extremely harmful results. If the values of the domestic society require that the *status quo* should eventually be changed, it follows that the enterprise can only be undertaken, if it can be undertaken at all, by indirect and untraditional means over a lengthy timescale. If traditional state diplomacy is powerless to achieve desirable objectives it need have no necessary objection to their attainment by alternative means, given that it accepts the desirability of the objectives, which it must if it is the faithful servant of the home society. The decline in the traditional strength of Britain, which produces a relatively powerless diplomacy, could thus have the effect of generating an extremely radical breed of diplomatists, eager for the achievement of international goals by non-diplomatic means in Europe and elsewhere.

Fourth, if the substance of diplomacy is the strength of the state deployed to further its foreign policy, it follows that actions taken by governments which have the effect of increasing their strength cannot be entirely repugnant to diplomacy. As suggested earlier, governmental transnationalism can be seen as increasing the strength of state by extending its capability to dislocate the actions of other states, by giving it extra leverage within alliances, and by presenting it with the possibility, at least, of deploying the strength of other states behind its own foreign policy. And, fifth, the intermingling of state instrumentalities in transnational systems cannot destroy foreign policy if the objectives of foreign policy, the achievement of safety, for example, are most nearly attained in this way, provided the state is able to exert its sovereignty by withdrawing from these entanglements if it judges its foreign policy objectives to be endangered by them.

The existence of points of contact such as these may substantiate a belief that by attending to practical problems as they arise, British governments will escape the direct impact of the doctrinal schism which lies beneath contemporary foreign policy. However, in the immediate past the traditional doctrine of foreign policy and diplomacy has constituted a brake on the British approach to governmental transnationalism and it may continue to do so.

CONCLUSION

The underlying institutional predicament of British foreign policy is created by differing interpretations of its own nature. At the level of practice, four sets of problems are distinguishable:

1. The general problem of the practicable level and nature of national

involvement required to achieve transnational order in particular systems, notably the economic system and the strategic system;

2. the particular problem of forming a coherent attitude to the transnational intergovernmental process in the European Community, which contains within it intimations of concentration on building a specific entity which could be destructive of transnational processes within wider international systems;

3. the problems of establishing links of complementarity and mutual support between different transnational intergovernmental organisations;

4. the problem of enmeshing the institutional instruments of national government with instruments of transnational government.

Discussion of these novel institutional problems is hampered by the continuing use of a language of international relations created by the myths and practices of sovereign statehood in an age of foreign policy transformation. This essay next turns to a consideration of some of the terms of this language in the modern setting.

Part Three   The vocabulary of foreign policy

7 Power

Adopting traditional assumptions, foreign policy can be seen as the struggle of the state to secure congenial actions from other states. The environment of the state is other states. Living agreeably in this environment depends on what other states do. Affecting what they do means exerting power and influence over them. The greater the strength of the state the more possible it is to deter and frighten potential enemies. In relations with allied states and with unaligned states, strength confers the ability to influence other foreign policies by a greater degree than they are able to influence one's own foreign policy.

Power and influence are the effects and the effectiveness of foreign policy. To be relatively effective in a particular international issue, foreign policy must be based on a strength greater than the strength of the other foreign policies comprising the issue. The greater the strength of the state, the wider is the range of issues in which it can exert relatively more power and influence than other states. The weaker the state the narrower is the area of its power and influence. Foreign policy operations are expenditures of strength which secure, or fail to secure, power and influence over the foreign policies of other states. The greater the available strength, the more freely may expenditures be made.

Strength is at the core of foreign policy. The resources of foreign policy comprise the strength of the state. Resources fall into a number of simple categories. First, there are those items which come under the general heading of geography. The larger the territory of the state, the more equable its climate, the more plentiful its mineral deposits, the more lush its soil, the greater is likely to be its strength. Within this category of geography may be included population: a large population confers more power than a small population provided it is not so

E

overblown that life at subsistence level is the common lot. Geography also covers foreign possessions and bases which add to the military and economic resources of the homeland.

A second broad category of state strength may be called mobilisation. A population without organised skills does not confer much power, nor do natural resources without capital and enterprise. Similarly, foreign bases and possessions cannot be exploited if skill and capital cannot be mobilised. Formidable military forces depend for their material and personnel on a homeland rich in skills and productive investment. Mobilisation is clearly a far from simple quality, intimately related as it is to the historical evolution of a particular community, its religious values, class structure, attitudes towards wealth and military strength, and its propensities to internal schism or general lassitude or to chauvinism and other forms of collective excitement.

A third aspect of strength, closely related to the other two categories, may be identified as government. This is the apparatus, formal and informal, whereby a community gives expression to a sense of direction, to the pursuit of internal and external goals. Determination, morale, efficiency, legitimacy are all included under the general heading of government. A form of government which does not benefit from a general sense of legitimacy or is grossly inefficient cannot be expected to make much of an impact on behalf of the state in its relations with other states. Government is a category which covers formal and informal apparatus; it also covers the nature of the actions of this apparatus. A form of government which is commonly given to a gross lack of realism and is incapable of matching its external policies and commitments to its capabilities, is also one which is unlikely to be able to exert power and influence over states whose governments are able to calculate their objectives more accurately and to maintain a practical accord between their objectives and the means available for their attainment. The capabilities of a state depend not merely on its geography and the extent to which its resources are mobilised, but also on government itself, on its form and on what it does. Government is the component which denotes a community's internal order and its capacity to pursue internal and external objectives with subtlety and efficiency. Government brings the internal and external circumstances of a given community into a stable balance which makes rational calculation and ordered expectations the norm of social life.

This kind of 'high' approach to the nature of foreign policy and the problems of government again conforms with widely held assumptions about the nature of strength and the ranking of states according to their power and influence. And this kind of intellectual apparatus is often used to explain the apparent decline of Britain in international society and to account for its foreign policy predicaments. Thus the power of the Soviet Union and the United States resides in their immense territories, formidable human and material resources, their highly mobilised economies and their coherent and positive forms of government. The weakness of Britain is accounted for by her small territory and population, her slender armed forces, and a certain irresolution on the part of her governments, which experience difficulty in accurately assessing their relatively weak capabilities and in formulating foreign policy objectives appropriate to them.

Given this kind of intellectual framework, Britain's former strength can be seen to have been based on geography in the sense that her homeland was rendered relatively secure by its surrounding moat, while her overseas empire compensated for her own relative weakness in terms of natural resources. Her population grew in a way adequate to the earlier stages of industrialisation, to which her relatively small size and good internal communications, together with her traditional concern with maritime trade, were distinct assets. Her geographical situation also naturally emphasised the place of naval strength in her external policies. This was a fairly inexpensive, politically untroublesome and flexible form of military endeavour. Forces which protected trade lanes required foreign bases, but these could be secured relatively easily while distant populations were backward and unmobilised and while other European powers were relatively defective in naval strength and prowess. In defending the homeland the navy could also blockade a substantial part of the European coastline in times of war. While the balance of power in Europe worked effectively, the European states concentrated on their continental concerns and did not undermine Britain as a maritime power. Britain could thus limit her European military involvement to occasional expeditionary forays whose aim was to tilt the continental balance against any potential hegemony on the part of a power hostile to Britain.

In the category of mobilisation, Britain accumulated and deployed capital earlier and more effectively than other European powers. She was also able to invest in the Empire and other relatively underdeveloped areas by virtue of the sense of security conferred on her investors by the general presence of the navy. She was thus able to mobilise natural resources overseas to compensate for her own poor endowments. The policy of free trade, again substantiated by the British navy, worked to her advantage while she dominated the world market for industrial products, and it made London pre-eminent among the world's trading and financial centres. Her currency, in local forms, was used within the Empire. The sterling area operated as a free financial market offering a flow of private investment to developing areas largely under British political control. The sterling system was responsive to trends (relating to interest rates, for example) at the centre: it was also responsive to central control in the sense that the British government exercised authority over local money supply and determined the level of local reserves. The mobilisation of an international economy in this way was matched by the direct military mobilisation of overseas resources. Local armies, most notably the Indian Army, were central to imperial strategy, and a large proportion of the costs, together with a proportion of the costs of maintaining naval bases, could be charged to local exchequers.

In the category of government, Britain also had a number of advantages: a long tradition of centralised rule, an unusual measure of internal political stability, a skilled and mobile society held in coherent form by a long-established nationalism, a reverence for class and status, and a fairly adaptable constitution able to bend to the political demands of new classes and new concentrations of internal wealth and influence. The apparatus of foreign policy was dominated by a small social elite which, as a rule, was able to react flexibly to external exigencies, unbound by fixed popular hatreds or crusades and relieved of the anxieties of indistinct national boundaries. Additionally, overseas affairs were divided into two distinct areas, foreign affairs and Empire, and later, Commonwealth affairs. Outside the Empire British governments had few ambitions and no claims in or on continental Europe, other than a general interest in the integrity of the Low Countries and in the maintenance of a condition of balance among the first-class European states. Otherwise Britain was concerned with the defence of the Empire and its communications and in generally working towards a condition of international relations in which Empire and Commonwealth might prosper. To this end British governments were later concerned to harmonise their interests with those of other non-European states, notably with the United States and Japan.

British power and influence waned as strength in all these categories was undermined by internal and external developments and by technological advances unrestricted to a particular territorial base. Geography changed most markedly. British strength was relative, and naturally declined, not in absolute terms but relatively to other industrialising states such as Germany, the United States, Japan and later Russia. Britain thus lost her dominance in industrial markets at a relatively early stage. The maintenance of naval strength and superiority became more expensive as weapons grew more complex. Also naval strength became less relevant to the defence of the homeland as continental Europe produced threats which called forth two massive military exertions in the space of thirty years. The policy of limited continental commitments collapsed entirely in face of the threat of continental hegemony by Germany and later by the Soviet Union. Technological developments, first air power, then nuclear missile power, shrank the British moat to strategic insignificance. The erosion of harmonisation with Japan, coupled with the effects of air power and submarine power on naval warfare, began to transform the Empire and Commonwealth from a source of geographical strength to one of geographical weakness through its complete deficiency in internal lines of communication and through its capacity to involve Britain in major distant conflicts while the homeland was gravely hazarded by continental threats.

In terms of mobilisation, as here defined, Britain also began to suffer a marked decline from the end of the nineteenth century. An economic network of domestic relations in the forefront of change during the first industrial revolution proved itself somewhat rigid and unadaptable in succeeding waves of technological advance. So Britain not merely lost ground in comparison with the rise of new industrial states with larger domestic bases, she also began to diminish in absolute terms as her economy became relatively uncompetitive, while her apparent hold over external Empire markets and sources of primary produce excited the hostility of other first-rank states. As luck would have it, the most essential new raw material, oil, was not an Empire asset. Moreover, the British ability to mobilise the Empire began to diminish with the growth of local nationalisms which Britain had neither the military strength nor the resolve to hold down in an age of popular democracy. The end of the Indian Empire, which removed the Indian Army from any calculation of British strength, made nonsense of the idea of the Empire and Commonwealth as a collective defence community. The transformation of the Empire also undermined the sterling area as a resource. As the result of British military exertions in the twentieth century large sterling balances were run up with colonial and Commonwealth governments. As imperial ties weakened these governments began to ignore rules regulating the use of these balances, regarding them as purely national resources. Sterling liabilities were vastly greater than Britain's gold and dollar reserves, so the collapse of central control of the sterling area and overseas sterling assets exposed her to acute balance of payments crises. The sterling area became more of a liability as British governments tried to maintain the confidence of sterling holders by offering exceptionally high rates of interest and by trying to guarantee sterling area governments against losses incurred as the result of sterling devaluations. And it was no longer possible to charge the costs of overseas defence establishments to local governments: indeed such establishments became a form of economic aid from Britain, dangerous in their potentiality for drawing her into distant conflicts she could ill afford to see through.

In the area of government, as here defined, the decline in British resources was even more marked. Popular democracy gained an iron hold on foreign policy not in a direct sense but through the domestic demands made upon government as a whole. The Victorian situation in which a large navy could be maintained while sections of the domestic population existed in conditions of acute squalor had disappeared by the middle of the twentieth century. Even the imposition of short periods of compulsory military service became a political liability which no government would readily endure. Economic growth, and the expansion of the social services which appeared to depend upon it, became an imperative of domestic politics and, slowly, of foreign policy too. Meanwhile the old flexibility of the foreign policy elite had disappeared, as had, temporarily at least, its power of psychological adaptation. The distinction between foreign affairs and Commonwealth affairs persisted after the reality behind it had changed. The sterling area ceased to be in the authoritative hands of central government and Britain was forced to rely on American assistance to maintain the credibility of her assets in the context of her sterling liabilities. Overall Commonwealth defence had also shown itself during the Second World War to be acutely dependent on American foreign policy and military strength, a fact duly acknowledged after the war by Australia and New Zealand in their emphasis on defence relations with the United States. The policy of harmonisation thus became one of stark dependence on the United States, not merely in Commonwealth terms but also in terms of the defence of Britain and Western Europe from the potential hegemony of the Soviet Union. Yet the maintenance of the sterling area and the defence of the Commonwealth and its communications remained high in government priorities, even though Britain had entered into apparently permanent and costly military commitments in Europe.

The illusion remained that Britain could be flexible in her foreign policy. The sterling and Commonwealth connections, coupled with the absolute priority of the Anglo-American relationship which these forced upon the British approach to the external world, conspired to prevent Britain from entering wholeheartedly into the early phases of the movement which resulted in the creation of the European Community. As the burden of the sterling area became more apparent than any benefits its existence might bestow on Britain, as Commonwealth defence after the Suez débâcle gradually began to seem merely a charge to Britain's inadequate economy, as Britain denied herself intimate relations with European countries growing economically stronger than herself, as the policy of harmonisation with the United States seemed to degenerate into comprehensive subservience with the decline and disappearance of the special relationship (which ceased to have emotional significance for American governments after the departure from office of President Eisenhower), so the thought began to occur that Britain really had emerged in the postwar world without a role and without a foreign policy of any distinctive kind. The decline of British power over enemies and influence over associates thus seemed complete. External circumstances combined with the inadequacies of British strength in terms of geography, mobilisation and government, had shattered the illusion of the flexibility of British foreign policy and the only recourse lay in lacklustre decisions to seek, and eventually to find, entry to the Community.

The power doctrine of foreign policy thus seems to have appreciable explanatory force when applied to the British experience. No political theory can avoid prescription and this one is no exception. If all foreign policy is to be equated with the exertion by the state of power and influence over other states, then British entry to the Community must be interpreted as an act of foreign policy of a traditional kind, whose purpose must be the reassertion of a distinctively British presence in international relations. By this action, therefore, the British state gains influence over the other Western European states through the mechanisms of the Community, and by the possibilities for disruption which these confer, which she should use as a method of asserting British foreign policy in Europe. It offers the possibility, at least, of finally liquidating the sterling area and providing Britain with the prospect of exerting a distinctive and forceful presence in international economic negotiations. Moreover, the Community confers a capability to influence the actions of the other members towards the rest of the world and thus enhances British power in this wider setting. In this way, for example, relations with the United States may be placed on a less dependent and more flexible footing. The British place in the Community, together with its developing independence of outside sources of energy as offshore sources of oil are exploited, may mean that the British state will be sought after for what it can do rather than indulgently supported because it can do nothing. Freed of the shackles of the Commonwealth and sterling area, the distinction between the British state and other states is now once more a clear one and military policy need not be burdened by the illusion of an impossible world responsibility. Instead it should concentrate on adding to Britain's influence over neighbouring states. To this end, it might be argued, persistence with the nuclear deterrent into the next generation of weapons will deny France military dominance in Western Europe, yield influence over West Germany, particularly in relation to her Eastern policies, and, perhaps, discourage the United States from using a monopoly position to create an overall strategic system in which the market for British favours entirely disappears.

POWER AND THE TRANSFORMATION OF FOREIGN POLICY

The power style of explaining the toils of modern British foreign policy is a clear and forceful one. The essential precepts of the power doctrine are that the state controls resources within the area of its direct jurisdiction, that these resources confer strength on the state, and that the state uses this strength to exert power and influence over other states. Changes in modern British foreign policy are thus explained in terms of the relative diminution of her strength since the end of the nineteenth century and of her consequently declining power in the international arena. From this viewpoint, the growth of transnationalism in all its manifestations has deepened the decline of British strength by raising formidable doubts about the control which British governments actually exercise over resources which appear to be within the boundaries of the state and by directly impeding Britain's deployment of her limited strength through the close involvement of transnational intergovernmental organisations in both her domestic and international actions.

The transformation of foreign policy may therefore be seen in terms of yet further erosions of British strength leading to yet more constraints on British governments. The reduction of Britain proceeds insidiously but particularly speedily by economic means. Given this outlook, multinational companies constitute a form of enterprise of ideological significance, since they may be readily seen as a collective threat to the authority of governments and to the basic autonomy of the state. They undermine the state's autonomy in three ways. First, decisions within multinational companies are inclined towards achieving economic goals over the whole field of their operations, which, by definition, are transnational. So the decisions of multinational companies with subsidiaries in Britain are not likely to be taken with exclusive reference either to the British economy or to nationalist requirements in Britain relating to autonomy or to other non-economic goals. Second, it is generally characteristic of multinational companies in Britain that the bulk of their research and development programmes are concentrated elsewhere, usually in their countries of historic origin. Thus, it may seem, Britain is deprived of the core resources of science and technology on which national industrial strength depends. Third, the great scale of multinational companies constitutes an intrinsic threat of monopolistic strength in a small market such as that provided by Britain, where they may seem generally to outrank smaller British companies. It may seem more a tragedy than an irony that this kind of perception, among many other pressures, has led British governments to see the merit of widening the British domestic market by merging with the European Community in order to provide the basis of growth in British companies and thus to increase their international competitive strength. Entry to the European Community increases the impact of transnationalism on British autonomy and sovereignty; so a threat to strength has been met by a further depletion of strength.

Besides undermining the basic material of national autonomy, multinational companies also appear to circumscribe the direct authority of British governments in three further ways. First, they challenge the meaning of some socialist governmental choices. A multinational company cannot be effectively nationalised by one national government. Foreign-owned subsidiaries in Britain can be taken over, but such a course has little substance when the viability of subsidiaries is dependent on a chain of production which is in no way limited to Britain and when the relevant centres of company decision-making and development effort are located abroad. Second, multinational companies are well placed to avoid some forms of national regulation. Taxation, for example, can be avoided because such companies can (though there is little evidence that they do) arrange their internal accounting in such a way as to register their profits in a country, and a currency, where taxation arrangements are most favourable to them. Third, a large multinational company, in its relations with a particular government, may have a greater bargaining strength than the government itself because it can arrange its investment programme in such a way as, for example, to deprive a development region of the prospect of much needed employment. In this sense governments often compete for the favours of multinational companies and their individual bargaining strength is diminished as a consequence. In global terms it is rare for countries, such as some oil-producing states, to combine to increase their strength and thus to extract massive benefits directly from the operations of multinational companies and to exercise direct international leverage through the medium of those operations.

The political effects of the growth of multinational companies excite almost as much comment as do the effects of transnational monetary movements, upon which this essay has already dwelt. They are manifestations of both an underlying transnational economy which seems to offer the prospect of wealth and of national decline simultaneously.

The existence of a massive international strategic system, dominated by the deterrence relationship of the first-rank powers, dwarfs Britain's military strength. Additionally, this system has had the effect upon what remains of this strength of creating a sense of doubt as to whether it can be called a national power resource at all. This additional, more fundamental, diminution of British military strength takes three broad forms. First, most of this strength is immersed in a transnational military alliance. This means that much of the training and command of British forces is orientated to the requirements of the alliance. The deeper this orientation, the less possible is it to use these forces outside the alliance for major international purposes to which the alliance itself is not adapted. Even though British units might be quickly withdrawn from the alliance by a British government, this basic socialisation would not suit them to independent use. Second, much of the equipment in use by British forces is produced transnationally. The more Britain pursues economy in its military strength and solidarity in its alliance policy, the greater this effect is likely to be. Third, in almost all conceivable circumstances, the more zealously Britain pursues continental defence (or security) the more foreigners are directly and intimately involved in the command, deployment and inspection of British forces.

The transformed nature of the milieu in which British governments attempt to act can thus be held to complete the dissolution of their power resources. This is not only an effect of the milieu itself; it is also an effect of the methods governments have been compelled to adopt to deal with its problems. The creation of transnational intergovernmental organisations of all kinds, military and economic, have opened the domestic arena to outside scrutiny and direct interference. They also commonly require direct commitments from British governments to consult with other governments, and even to secure their positive approval, before using the scant power that remains to them.

THE OMISSIONS OF POWER

The power explanation of modern British foreign policy is not un-flawed. A cursory examination of the data of recent experience quickly reveals factors which are not fully explicable in the language of power.

First, it is far from certain that British governments and foreign policy elites invariably regarded the Commonwealth and sterling area as British resources which were a bitter disappointment when they turned out to be liabilities. It is at least arguable that these associations were regarded partly as a form of service to the international community and to humanity at large. Nor can this view be lightly dismissed. The sterling area was an asset to the underdeveloped countries included among its members. It gave them access to a large capital market and it provided them with a medium whereby they might increase their international trade. Britain's sterling liabilities constituted a pool of liquidity which they could use to finance deficits, and Britain's efforts to maintain the dollar values of these assets could be interpreted as both acts of honour and as a form of direct overseas aid. Similarly, the Commonwealth was partly viewed, not as a colonialist hangover but as an exercise in international, multiracial association. After the Second World War it imposed few burdens on its members other than Britain, and by its nature it drew new countries into partnership with more developed countries. It was a model of how the developed and underdeveloped parts of the world should conduct their relations. It adapted the nation state in order to lessen its propensities for conflict, while in no way infringing the dignity or authority of national governments. And it drew smaller developed countries, like Australia, into an awareness of the full international environment and offered them a role both in relation to the economically backward countries and to the states of the North Atlantic, through their influence on Britain. The military significance of the Commonwealth in the post-war world was not that it contributed to the first-rank pretensions of British politicians, but that it represented both a debt of honour acquired by Britain in two European wars and a human responsibility to provide conditions of security in which new countries could move towards their own version of modernity in peace. Thus the British military role in the long Malayan emergency was the modest one of general service to local stability and independence, not the manic assertion of an impossible military dominance in Asia.

Second, it might be contended that the image of Britain in deluded pursuit of power and influence from a position of fading national strength ignores the very real measure of internationalism which British governments manifested. Britain participated prominently in the founding of the IMF in partnership with the United States (at the time there were very few other powers with whom partnership was possible) in the cause of international economic order and the control of national economic sovereignty. British proposals to this end, relating, for example, to the placing of burdens of adjustment on surplus countries, would have rendered the IMF a far more relevant and powerful body than it turned out to be. Nevertheless, Britain subsequently played the game under the new rules of the dollar exchange system, providing the world, reluctantly perhaps, with a pool of sterling liquidity and allowing other countries devastated by war, particularly Japan and West Germany, to maintain low exchange rates which enabled them to acquire a general surplus on their balance of payments. Whatever else it may have been, it could reasonably be argued that this was not a policy of national aggrandisement.

Thirdly it may be argued that British policies towards Europe were not those of a state determined to maintain its national independence and its power base in the world at large. The commitment of a sizeable proportion of British forces to an almost indefinite presence in Germany under Nato command represented an act of continental responsibility which conferred few immediate political benefits on Britain, and on which Britain was required to expend foreign currency she could ill afford. This was not an act of international dominance but of European and Atlantic partnership. Similarly, it might be argued that British non-participation in the higher flights of the European movement was in no way a policy of retaining national power but the reflection of the British concern for Western unity as a whole. The longstanding doctrine of the three interlocking circles (Western Europe, the Commonwealth, and the Anglo-American relationship) as the basis of postwar British foreign policy can be interpreted as a doomed attempt to muster these three elements of international society to the maintenance of her own status and strength. But it was a doctrine which could also be interpreted as the manifestation of a British concern for the creation of a Western Community, which, apart from its own intrinsic value, would, for example, be responsible and disinterested in its treatment of the underdeveloped world. If such an aim were to be achieved Britain could not lock itself into a regional movement which would emphasise discontinuities in a world which morally and materially demanded the establishment of continuities within the group of Western industrialised nations and between this group and the underdeveloped countries. Similarly, Britain exerted itself in the Anglo-American partnership at the height of the Cold War to modify the harsher ideological aspects of American foreign policy and to urge the merits of a Soviet–American dialogue.

It is thus possible to see recent British foreign policy not as the story of declining strength making nonsense of frantic efforts to assert the sovereign power of the state, but as the record of the struggles of British governments to harmonise their internal and external responsibilities, to participate in the complexities of international government and politics from a field of increasingly demanding domestic politics. British governments were not so much obsessed by the concept of the state as by the network of national and international responsibilities and influences of which they were a part.

THE IRRELEVANCE OF POWER

If the concept of power is less than adequate to the explanation of British foreign policy seen as the specifically foreign actions of the state, its propensity to explain the changing structure of foreign policy simply as the continuing diminution of the strength of the state is substantially irrelevant. This transformation takes two basic forms. First, the intimate mixing of the domestic and the foreign settings of government and politics has had the effect of dissolving the notion of resources of strength which are purely national. In its place must be put a far more complex notion of the transnational resources of international systems. From this viewpoint, the Western international economy, for example, does not undermine the resources of Britain;

Britain participates in the resources of the Western international economy. This participation carries with it the concomitant disadvantage of involvement in the disturbances of a system which is conterminous with an imperfect political order. Second, many of the international actions of governments consequently become efforts to improve the international political order and to render governable intractable transnational systems. These efforts cannot be seen simply as applications of national power to the foreign policies of other governments. Efforts to maximise the resources of the international economy and to limit its propensities to instability through transnational intergovernmental organisations, are not expenditures of power but the application of the authority of governments to underlying transnational social problems. The application of national economic power in disputes between governments, though it clearly takes place, is irrelevant to this more difficult task, which is of fundamental importance to both industrial countries and to the developing countries linked with them.

This attitude to power can even be applied to the most harsh of manifestations of traditional national strength, military force. The Atlantic defence community, to which British governments have long been committed, confers the obvious benefit on Britain of cheap defence through deterrence. The abridgement of the strictly national control of British military forces in this community cannot be regarded as a diminution of British power if British governments wish to maintain defence in the nuclear age. The objective, defence, renders irrelevant the strictly national control of military forces. If defence is successful, how can it also be argued to diminish Britain? Similarly, practical efforts to stress collective defence through transnational armaments programmes do not look like reductions in British strength if they constitute the economical means of maintaining a community essential to British safety. An increase in collective defence cannot be equated with a loss of British strength. What is increased is not equal to what is decreased. An increase in transnational defence is also an increase in British defence.

This kind of approach can be taken a step further. British involvement in a transnational defence community is only a part of Britain's participation in the milieu of prospective destruction. In a broader perspective British governments are also participants in the strategic system of deterrence as a whole, which intertwines large patterns of international conflict and cooperation. Participation in this system imposes two costs on Britain: first, the cost of the British contribution to the Atlantic defence community, which is a part of the overall strategic system; and, second, the overwhelming prospective cost in terms of destruction should the whole system's tendency to instability become so extreme as to result in nuclear war. A logical method of reducing these costs, discussed in earlier chapters, is through a policy of security which might lessen the system's instability to the eventual point at which the actual cost of defence might become unnecessary and at which the potential cost of strategic breakdown might disappear. It has been suggested earlier that this goal could be served by the creation of a new European Security Organisation to which national forces might be committed. Assuming that such an enterprise actually represents an advance towards the goal of security, to suggest that the allocation of British forces to it would constitute a further diminution of British strength is irrelevant to the issue, which is the achievement of security. If the goal of security, or something approaching it, is achieved, then Britain benefits through a growth in the governability of the international strategic system of which she is a part. This cannot be viewed in terms of a loss of strength. If British governments became committed to a policy of security, and if they could begin to achieve something of the kind through a new transnational European organisation, then their security policy would be a successful one. The traditional power explanation of foreign policy asserts that power is exerted to further national policies. But if policies which are international rather than national in nature are furthered by the merging of strengths, then the traditional explanation may be deemed to refer to a condition of international relations which does not actually exist. The achievement of security would add to the powers of British governments by providing them with a more peaceful environment in which to operate and by releasing to them resources otherwise devoted to defence.

Transnational organisations can thus be seen as occupying a position of complementarity, not competitiveness, with national governments. This aspect of the changing structure of foreign policy may be further demonstrated by the examples of transnational organisation in the international monetary system. If the IMF could be reconstituted in such a way as to make it capable of both allocating burdens of adjustment and of controlling the overall supply of reserve assets, then it would undoubtedly be a more powerful body. But in what senses would a more powerful IMF reduce the powers of British governments? As a country given to balance of payment deficits, the equitable allocation of burdens of adjustment is presumably in the British interest. If Britain could finally liquidate the international reserve role of sterling, then British governments would be relieved of a burden which has long been deemed a constraint on their freedom of action; the removal of this burden would consequently increase their effectiveness. If a transnational body such as the IMF could make an impact on international inflationary pressures through the control of world money supplies, then it would follow that government anti-inflationary policies in Britain might have a higher chance of success than they can have when international inflation is not subject to general control. Again, the effectiveness of British governments would be increased.

This kind of complementarity even extends to non-governmental actors in the transnational setting. Multinational companies contribute to the British economy by importing into it managerial and technological innovation and by creating needed employment (Scotland and Wales are major beneficiaries of this kind of transnational activity). The objectives of British governments in seeking to increase British wealth and competitiveness are not therefore in necessary conflict with the interests of multinational companies. Moreover, such companies engaged in the oil industry need the cooperative involvement of governments of consuming countries as much as those countries need oil. Harmful effects in terms of monopoly, foreign control of research and suchlike, can be met in part by encouraging the growth of more British direct foreign investment through the multinational expansion of British companies. As, and if, multinational companies as a whole grow to the point at which they constitute a serious impediment to the effectiveness of governments, then clearly a general motivation will develop to create appropriately transnational intergovernmental supervisory and regulatory organisations. To interpret such a development as a further sacrifice of national strength on the altar of transnationalism would be to miss the point. Governments would be seeking to make themselves more effective, not less effective, in changing world conditions through the institution of complementary governmental services at the transnational level at which multinational companies move.

CONCLUSION

The course of modern British foreign policy can be described in terms of the inexorable decline of British national strength and of British

exertions to compensate for the resulting loss of power. Accepting its
assumptions, this explanation is at best only partial. If British foreign
policy is undergoing not a decline but a transformation, the assumptions of this explanation become largely irrelevant, and explanations
in terms of the complementarity of national and transnational government takes its place.

8 Democracy

Theories of democracy are oddly reticent about problems of foreign policy, the problems of the democratic community immersed in international society, though democratic practice and argument are often deeply absorbed in just these problems. A democratic community, such as Britain, is an open community, whose relations with its milieu are complex and numerous; so it would seem to be a duty of the democrat to attempt to formulate a view of democracy which addresses itself to the real conditions of the open community.

Debate on foreign policy and democracy commonly stresses three sorts of issues. First, there are the questions concerning the actual substance of foreign policy operations. What is a democratic foreign policy, what does it do that is distinctively democratic? Does it favour the establishment of international organisations and obedience to their allocations, even though some other members may not be markedly democratic? Does it attempt to undermine foreign governments which are undemocratic? Does the democratic state simply concentrate on defending itself and on furthering its own national interests without external concern for distinguishing itself as a democracy?

Second, there are the issues raised by the strongly executive nature of traditional foreign policy. To what extent should a government be allowed to operate internationally free from domestic democratic control? How should the democrat respond to the possibility that the executive may gain additional domestic power by virture of its international competence and actions? To what degree should a democratic government impose duties on the domestic community in fulfilment of international agreements which that community has not willed in the form of domestic legislation? To what extent can and should the foreign policy process be opened to democratic participation?

Third, there are the related, but nevertheless novel, problems created by the transformation of foreign policy, by the growth of transnational systems of relations and by the proliferation of transnational intergovernmental organisations. What is the domestic legitimacy of decisions, however mild in form, enacted at the transnational level? This problem is most vividly presented by the European Community, which, acting principally through the Council of Ministers, has a limited legislative authority over the citizens of the United Kingdom. In practice, so far, the Council shows a tender regard for the wishes of each government in the exercise of this authority. To the degree that the Council observes unanimity, the democratic problem it raises may be argued to fall under the second category, that of enhancing the domestic power of the executive through its primacy in the external environment. But in principle the Council of Ministers can move by weighted majority. What is the democratic status of Community legislation in Britain which has been passed in the face of the opposition of the British government? Less dramatically, the growth of transnational intergovernmental activity may be seen to have increased the bureaucratic influence on authoritative decision-making. This characteristic is also most notably, though not uniquely, present in the European Community because of the central role it ascribes to the European Commission and because of this body's close cultivation of national bureaucracies.

Liberal democracy has no settled definition, nor can it have if it is to remain liberal. In order to investigate these foreign policy problems this essay reduces theories of democracy to two schools: the code school and the group school. The first school emphasises the formal requirements and institutions of democracy; the second emphasises the political structure of democracy, its political processes, adjustments and arguments.

FOREIGN POLICY AND CODE DEMOCRACY

A generally accepted requirement of the code school is that in a democracy there must be regular elections, at which governments, prospective governments and political representatives of all kinds, compete for votes. Subject to disqualification on grounds of criminality, insanity and suchlike, votes are cast by all adults in the community and each voter has the same number of votes. Through elections voters control the group (not necessarily all the individuals) which is to occupy governmental roles. Between elections governments are subjected to all kinds of influences and pressures, but at elections they may be dismissed. If elections are to control representation and government, it follows that there can be no limitation on the number of candidates or parties at elections. The responsiveness of representatives to public opinion, and other more exact pressures, is ensured by the prospect of their having to face free elections. Representation is not government. Some representatives will not be in the government nor will they support the government. But they will accept the decision of the majority of representatives pending the next election, at which the minority will exert itself to become a majority.

In this basic model of the code school's view of democracy, rule and representation are related to elections at which rulers and representatives may be removed, their roles exchanged, and newcomers installed or forestalled. What challenge to this method does the existence of foreign relations present?

If the traditional view of foreign policy approximates at all closely to reality, then one is drawn to the conclusion that foreign policy need upset democracy very little. If international relations comprise a distinctly interstate arena in which a representative government can act, or decline to act, as an independent self-directing entity, it would seem to follow that a given government could be held appropriately responsible for its foreign actions at elections, when an alternative government, offering a range of alternative foreign policies, may be installed in its place. The bias towards the executive which this kind of foreign policy implies must be met between elections by the endeavours of citizens and representatives to open international politics to public scrutiny and debate so that the nature of the executive's record may be fully appreciated.

But if this traditional notion of international relations is rejected complications begin to appear. Let us move to the opposite pole and suggest that the democratic citizen is subjected to a large number of forces, official and unofficial ,emanating from abroad, which lie substantially beyond the control of his own government. In other words a democratic government cannot rule the area of public affairs as it affects the citizen, only part of it. So at elections voters do not elect their government, because they are, to a degree, governed by the actions of external governments, and the strict relationship between rulers and elections established in the simple code model of democracy no longer holds.

A purely theoretical response to the central democratic problem of this model immediately presents itself. National governments should be fused into an international government able to rule in the whole area of public affairs as they affect citizens. This international government would be subject to the periodic discipline of elections and the code school would be broadly satisfied. This logical resort need not be dwelt on: its remoteness resides in a number of obvious factors, prominent among which is the fact that free elections are by no means a universally accepted, understood or feasible means of appointing rulers and representatives.

Intermediate positions come a little closer to reality. There is no reason why an elected European Community government and parliament, which are indistinct objectives of the Community programme, should not be properly democratic in the code sense. As yet the Community is very far from this goal. The governments of the Community still regard the main area of their mutual contacts as a special kind of highly bureaucratised diplomacy. Yet the legislative consequences of this kind of diplomacy can affect the lives of citizens in a detailed fashion. This characteristic of the Community can be seen to raise the general dilemma of democratic foreign policy when the distinction between domestic affairs and international affairs becomes unreal: this is the non-coincidence of authority and democratic responsibility. If the European Council of Ministers were to adhere very closely to the principle of unanimity in its operations, its impact on the code model of democracy need not be severe, because in these circumstances the decisions of the Council would be decisions of the British government in a very exact sense. Although decisions taken in this way might be argued to enhance the power of the executive, provided the executive is subjected to public scrutiny it can be held fully responsible at elections for all its actions and policies and no great injury is done to the democratic code. At an election an alternative government might offer to reverse European policies, and on return to office, exerting the principles of sovereignty and unanimity to the full, promptly dissociate itself from the positions of its predecessors in the Council of Ministers. The results of this kind of assertion of the democratic code might be twofold: first, to maintain the absolutely central position of the Council of Ministers in the Community, preventing any kind of authority being shared with other European institutions; and, secondly, to introduce such an element of uncertainty, and ultimately of disorder, into the affairs of the Council of Ministers as to undermine its continuity and cripple the programme of the Community.

Let us suppose that activities such as these are generally uncongenial to British governments, that they are prepared to accept Community decisions with which they do not wholly agree, and that they would not be eager to repudiate earlier Community decisions made during the tenure of previous British governments. The more that responses to the Community take this kind of form, the more, it would seem, the code model is infringed, because government and elections are not exactly matched. British citizens, to a minor degree, are governed by an authority which they do not wholly elect.

However, it is not immaterial to this problem that the governments of each of the other Community countries are, for the present, democratic, and may be held to conform broadly to the code model. So any case made in relation to Britain applies equally to the other countries of the Community. Given, then, that voting in Community institutions is weighted to account for differences of population size, much of the democratic code can still be held to apply. For if one takes the view that a British government in this setting is not wholly a governing body, but a representative of British voters, then it is unexceptional to note that occasionally it should be pressed into uncongenial policies. Representatives, in the nature of their situation, do not get things all their own way. According to the model, representatives accept decisions of the majority, provided the majority is properly elected. As we have seen, the governments of the Community countries are elected, so a Community majority is a proper one.

This kind of argument might be held to show that the problem of democratic foreign policy, in this example, is not really a problem, were it not that an element of the code model is the dismissibility of representatives and governments at elections. Ministers of democratic governments coming together in the Community to decide a matter affecting the lives of citizens act as a sort of combined legislature and executive. But this limited and unusual kind of government is not dismissible as a whole. The parts of it (the Dutch part, the German part and so on) are dismissible at elections. But the body as a whole does not fall into this category, nor can it until such time as European elections are held and a European executive is made fully responsible to the European Parliament.

A further difficulty, which will be touched on at a later stage, relates to the European Commission. To the degree to which this appointed body is simply the administrative arm of the Council of Ministers, the democratic problems it raises can be subsumed under those created by the Council itself. But it is formally an initiating body. To the degree to which it fulfils this role it raises a special problem. This is formally covered by the provision that it may be dismissed by the European Parliament, which is an elected body in the sense that, broadly, its members are elected to the assemblies of the constituent countries, though, like the members of the Council of Ministers, they are not all elected at the same time. However, since the distinction between the Council and the Commission is not in practice a clear one, it is difficult to know what actions of the Community it might be held responsible for. Just such a criticism might, of course, be directed at the senior members of the British civil service who have direct influence on the initiation and execution of government policies, but who are not elected and are not dismissible in any directly democratic sense. This kind of problem can be tackled, not entirely effectively, by ignoring the power of dismissal in relation to civil servants and by insisting, alternatively, that elected representatives be admitted, in the normal course of their duties, to an early stage of the policy-making process, so that bureaucrats cannot exercise power unobserved and uncriticised. Since the political importance of ministerial responsibility is not pressing at the Community level (no individual elected minister is responsible for a Commission proposal) there is no reason why the Commission should not be more open in this respect (both to enquiries in the European Parliament and in national assemblies such as the House of Commons) than is, for example, the British administrative apparatus in the domestic political setting.

Participation

The stark voting model of democracy is not one which commands universal respect among theorists or practitioners of democracy Democracy seen as a method to which no particular ends are attached disturbs the democratic conscience in its neglect of the moral quality of social life. Variants of the code model commonly attempt to correct this deficiency, first, by elaborating the relationship between the elector and his representatives; and, second, by attempting to delineate the nature of policies properly acceptable to the democrat. Here we shall simply examine one example of each of these two variants of the code model of democracy in relation to foreign policy.

Democracy may be argued to be a condition of involvement or participation. From this standpoint, when one refers to democracy one is referring not merely to the mechanisms of elections and governmental responsibility, but to a society in which democratic citizens participate actively in their own government. In a sense, democracy should be a form of moral education. By pressing the participating citizen to consider the impact on the community of particular authoritative choices, democracy encourages him to place his personal interests in the context of the interests of all. Thus the democratic citizen is placed in the morally demanding role of political trustee for his society.

The active citizen of the true democracy should be concerned in all matters of public importance, including, one assumes, foreign policy. Participation in foreign policy is morally enhancing in two ways: first, in the ordinary sense that acts of foreign policy can affect the whole community and the participating citizen must assess their nature and impact in this full light; second, foreign policy participation can take him to an even higher moral rung, for foreign policy operations affect international society and the participator must now consider the general wellbeing on a universal basis. The morally enhancing quality of foreign policy participation must, of course, be balanced against the morally dubious compromises and inconsistencies which the necessities of traditional statecraft may require in a world where what is moral and what is prudent do not always coincide.

There are a number of cogent objections to the concept of democracy as general participation. It may be contended, for example, that democratic rule is dependent on the existence, and the social standing, of large numbers of politically apathetic citizens whose democratic zeal is largely exhausted by casting their votes at elections. This is so, first, because order and governmental effectiveness demand that the excitements and distractions of popular arousal should be limited, so far as possible, to periodic elections; and, second, because mass involvement means mass politicisation, and in the twentieth century this has often been achieved along totalitarian lines. The notion that a popularly approved foreign policy was also a peaceful and democratic foreign policy did not long survive the rise of Hitler. It can be contended that the most valuable feature of life in a democracy is that a citizen may occupy his private domain broadly as he wishes. It follows from this that he must be free to exclude politics and foreign policy from his life. This is important both for himself and his society, because politics is dominated by politicians, and the indifference of large numbers of people to politicians may be an important protection against them.

A second set of objections draws its validity from the traditional view of foreign policy and diplomacy. It has often been argued that the relations between states do not form the proper material of continual democratic participation and control. For one thing, popular attitudes sometimes fall little short of a chauvinist bigotry which in itself is the antithesis of international negotiation. As well, international bargaining is a particularly subtle business. It may, for example, seem appropriate for diplomacy to adopt an extremely inflexible attitude until a particular negotiation is well advanced, when a reassessement may be undertaken as the result of concessions from the other side. The intrusion of massive public debate and pressure into such a delicate process may delay the formulation of an initial position almost indefinitely; and when, through the rack, an initial democratic position emerges, it may subsequently prove impossible to abandon, having become associated with the popular will and national honour. Similarly, it may be argued that when the arena of diplomacy is apparently democratised by the creation of open international organisations, like the League of Nations, wherein a quasiparliamentary style is deemed appropriate to the conduct of international politics, the resulting flood of rhetoric and unrealism deceives and confuses the democratic citizen and destroys the prudent and quiet authority of the traditional diplomat.

A third group of objections, also partly practical, refers to the available techniques of participation. It may be contended that the individual citizen is best able to involve himself in the detail of public affairs at the local level, where he is in a position to be fairly fully informed and thus able to offer distinctive contributions to authoritative actions whose results he may be as well placed as anyone to calculate. Assuming this to be the case, it does not follow that the individual citizen should participate in the formulation and execution of traditional foreign policy and diplomacy, if only because of the normally limited nature of his experience.

Participation in the usual run of domestic affairs is organised along familiar pressure group lines, which in the British case are usually institutionalised in political and administrative practices. But a broad distinction may be drawn between the domestic political system as it touches on domestic issues and as it touches on traditional high foreign policy and diplomacy. Almost any domestic issue is a matter of concern to a large number of highly involved groups, often with unchallengeable expert knowledge, which have recognised channels of communication to local authorities, political parties at all levels, to parliamentarians, to the administrative establishment, and to ministers.

This is the medium in which the detailed substance of domestic political issues is suspended. The domestic context of traditional foreign policy has a very different structure. Some of the most important issues of foreign policy (the reform of the international monetary system, the nature of the deployment of nuclear weapons by Nato, the relative commitment of the United Kingdom to various international organisations, and so on), though they may be of the utmost importance, are not profoundly enmeshed in the participatory structure of democracy in Britain.

On this observation can be founded the case that the foreign policy system is distinct in kind from the domestic policy system. There are relatively few groups constantly concerned with foreign policy issues; and many of those that are so concerned concentrate on single questions (like the possession of nuclear weapons, or the support or otherwise of racialist governments overseas) often at a high emotional pitch. Groups such as these are not intimately and expertly involved in the daily conduct of foreign affairs as a whole. Because of their crusading concentration on single issues abstracted from the total pattern of foreign policy, it can be argued that when they are not ineffective they distort. Because of the executive-dominated nature of foreign policy, they must aim to be effective at the top of the political pyramid. But assailed crudely and directly, this is perhaps the least open and malleable part of the political system. The individual citizen wishing to be active in traditional foreign affairs is not confronted by a highly complex system of groups and institutions extending from the local to the national level. He is a lonely fellow, doomed to writing books and consorting with zealots to whom the practical intricacy of international relations means little.

Because the individual citizen is relatively so isolated from the conduct of foreign affairs, it may be argued that the proper resort of the democratic codist is the institution of the referendum. By frequent referenda the democratic citizen is drawn directly into the matter of foreign policy. He is directly consulted on all important issues.

The referendum is not universally approved by democratic theorists of the codist persuasion and it has, as yet, no place in the British constitution. The democratic code here under discussion is concerned with the election of persons, who are in turn responsible for actual policies or for the framing of alternative policies. A referendum does not conform with this characteristic of the code. It is concerned with the direct approval, or otherwise, of particular items of policy. But the body approving such an item, the citizens participating in the referendum, is not dismissible. Second, questions selected for referenda are, as a rule, selected, timed, and phrased by governments which, in these circumstances, may reasonably be expected to get the answers they require. In this way the regular referendum contributes to an authoritarian kind of rule, which places itself above the stress and pressure of ordinary politics by its direct appeals to the citizenry. Thirdly, referenda oversimplify, they reduce the complex field of politics to a few questions requiring determinate answers. It may be contended that such a reduction to simplicity is a gross distortion of political actuality and to require the democratic citizen to be a party to it demeans him. And, fourthly, the referendum is particularly inappropriate to foreign affairs, where the sensitivity of foreigners is a fundamental part of the governmental field of action, which cannot be expected to become more tractable under the impact of broadsides from the national citizenry at large.

Many of these difficulties of democratic participation refer directly to the formulation and execution of high policy. If foreign policy is becoming progressively mixed with domestic policy, as has been contended here, then many of these difficulties become less acute. As the structure of domestic politics comes to include in its ordinary processes a concern for 'low' foreign policy, and as it is extended directly into the external arena (the Confederation of British Industry, for example, has quasidiplomatic representation of its own at Brussels) then the citizen is confronted by a political environment in which his domestic participation in group politics and pressures automatically includes an involvement in foreign affairs. This is not only so in the sense that some groups are directly active in the extranational environment. Participation in the domestic political process must also draw groups into expert involvement in the transnational concerns and obligations of democratic government.

Democratic policy

The second variant of the code school is one which addresses itself to the kinds of actions with which a democratic government should concern itself. From this viewpoint, the mark of democracy is not merely a code of rules relating to elections, but the nature of the actions which properly elected governments can, or should, undertake. Democracy is favoured because democratic governments are less likely than other governments to circumscribe the rights of the citizen. Democracy, the technique, is thus associated with values which transcend technique. Taking one example, from a range of possibilities, of this kind of approach to code democracy, let it be assumed that individual liberty is the primary value in social life, and that liberty is enjoyed by the man who, in Hayek's formulation, 'is not subject to coercion by the arbitrary will of another or others'.* It is also a requirement of this conception of liberty that coercion, of whatever kind, is reduced to a minimum. The importance of liberty rests on the premiss that the individual must have the maximum freedom possible to explore the potentialities of his own life and to pursue his personal interests, provided he does not transgress the rule of liberty by coercing others.

In this view the complexity of man in society is so great that no human mind can have the knowledge to substantiate a blueprint for man and society. The actions of government should not, therefore, attempt to determine the nature of society itself. Similarly, since all men, including politicians, are motivated by a degree of self-interest which they cannot themselves determine, no one has the right to legislate in more than a small area of human relations. Because the future of society cannot be known, it is the right of all men to investigate the potentialities of society to meet human needs. In the nature of the case, individual mistakes will be made, so caution and prudence are to be recommended; but all men should have the right to pursue their own paths to the maximum extent of their energies. This kind of freedom requires variety and complexity in society; in return it confers adaptability and resilience on society, and offers ever wider scope for self-fulfilment to individuals of later generations.

Government must concern itself with the safety of citizens, the prevention of crime, and the alleviation of any harmful effects arising from the large-scale enjoyment of individual choice. Law must be general, impersonal, and drawn up before application. Democracy is the preferred means of securing liberty because it emphasises individual equality and individual choice, at least at elections. The long-term majority principle, enshrined in well-spaced elections, is a counter-force to ephemeral majorities produced by the excitements of short-term emotive issues. The long-term majority is likely to find its ultimate expression in a consensus on the fundamental principles of

* F. A. Hayek, *The Constitution of Liberty*, Routledge, 1960, p. 11. The remarks which follow make no attempt to adhere closely to Hayek's work, which makes few references to foreign policy.

individual liberty, and thus form a barrier against arbitrary rule. The consensus may express itself through democracy, but it is not the simple product of the rules of voting. It is founded on the many social institutions of a free society, which, consequently, must be tampered with as little as possible.

The impact of this kind of thinking on foreign policy takes a number of not entirely consistent forms. It is clearly a primary duty of democratic government to resist the imposition on free citizens of alien rule by undemocratic governments which do not respect the value of liberty. At the same time, wars and imminent threats of wars should be avoided, because they clearly lead governments to ignore the domain of the individual by the close regulation of the economy, drafting the populace into various forms of war service, by passing large numbers of regulations, and, *in extremis*, acting in a thoroughly arbitrary fashion, by the use of powers of internment and the like. The implication of this is that governments should exert themselves to establish a working system of security whereby the threat of war can be reduced.

Yet in the foreign policy arena governments must be watched most closely, for it is here that the executive traditionally moves free from the day-to-day discipline of the legislative process in an elected assembly. The actions of the executive abroad may lead it to infringe the principles of abstraction and generality in the domestic environment: the foreign activities of American presidents have, arguably, led them to intrude too personally and too arbitrarily in American domestic affairs. This general danger of traditional external policy is heightened by the growing scope of modern transnational commitments. The British entry to the European Community subjects British citizens to a legislative process taking place abroad. To the degree which the Community operates in a diplomatic manner, it confers on the British executive the power to legislate by means of concealed machinations with foreign rulers. And the degree to which the Brussels machinery is dominated by an unelected bureaucracy is a measure of its further threat of arbitrary rule.

On the more positive side, an adherent to the views under discussion would, one assumes, recommend to government that foreign economic policy should aim to maximise the free movement of goods and resources, and so to restrain as little as possible natural human exertions in the pursuit of material wealth. Free trade, floating exchange rates, the free movement of gold and capital, these are the kinds of policies, or, more accurately, non-policies, which are likely to seem attractive to this school of thought. By these means, economic choices are maximised, both at home and abroad, international communications are encouraged, and the arbitrary powers of government are minimised.

Further, if internal policies are to be dominated by the imperative value of individual liberty, then consistency requires that the same value should dominate external policy. Though individual liberty depends in part on slowly evolved social structures and is not therefore possible of achievement in many parts of the world, the value itself remains valid. So, for example, foreign aid directed to immoderate governments in underdeveloped countries (which politicises economic decisions in these countries and increases the patronage and power of leaders to whom individual liberty is of little interest) is to be deplored. Far better that such countries be given access to world trade and capital markets, possibly on a preferential basis, so that internal economic choices may be increased and centres of wealth and enterprise outside government circles be created, and the ultimate end of the propagation of liberty served thereby.

In the matter of transnational organisations, this view of democracy need not be as disapproving as might first appear. The requirement that law should be kept to a minimum and be general and clear in its application, does not necessarily turn the democrat of this persuasion entirely against transnational machinery of the kind established in the European Community, even though he is likely to view the quasi-diplomatic nature of this legislative apparatus with some suspicion. Provided the regulations emanating from Brussels conform to the requirements of law in a free society, the fact that they are manufactured in a peculiar way is secondary. If laws are modest in their social intentions and general in their application the fact that they are oddly produced should be of relatively little significance. If, additionally, it can be shown that the existence of the Community widens the social and economic choices of the individual, and increases the range and subtlety of society as a whole, then its existence must be deemed to serve liberty.

In the general matter of international organisation, the democrat, as here defined, cannot claim possession of a blueprint of the future of world society. Clearly, prudence must be exercised in international undertakings. Liberties already enjoyed must not be lightly hazarded. But, by the nature of his beliefs, the democrat must tend to favour variety in government as in everything else. The simple government is likely to be the most inflexible, restrictive, socially distorting and, perhaps, arbitrary government. For reasons such as these, the democrat is generally favourable towards federal forms of government. At the international level, the federation of the countries of Western Europe (or of the world at large) is not immediately practicable. But as a general goal, undogmatically pursued, it is in no way inimical to liberty, perhaps the reverse, in its concern for the creation of a complex and various form of government. Cautious experimentation along these lines, provided the present enjoyment of liberty is not curtailed, is, one would think, to be encouraged by the democrat.

In the same way, the future government of international society at large is best investigated through a variety of institutions. Inconsistencies among these institutions (for example, between traditional diplomacy and the Community method, or between Nato and the UN) is in no way deplorable. The democrat is instinctively suspicious of neatness, or of the ideal of neatness in politics. Creative politics investigates the potentialities of men for variety with order. This conception demands an adaptive approach to the future, one which does not allow itself to be encased in existing institutions and inherited dispositions, though these demand a tender respect.

Individual democrats should be aware of the duties of liberty and should concern themselves with its values in and through foreign policy. They should propound concepts and arguments favourable to liberty on as wide a scale as possible, should cultivate as large a range of international contacts as they can, should generally regulate their lives in such a way as to bear testimony to the creativity and universality of liberty. A similar boldness cannot be expected of governments, whose special responsibilities for order and safety place them in a position requiring a particular circumspection. But the relationship of the bold individual and the cautious government is a vital one in democratic foreign policy.

GROUP VERSIONS OF DEMOCRACY: THE DEMOCRATIC ELITE

We turn next to theories which focus on the nature of political behaviour in a democracy. The first example in this category stresses both the claimed fact and the claimed merit of elite rule.

Theorists of this persuasion point to two basic observations which appear to undermine the notion of democracy as popular participation and control. First, the level of political interest and knowledge among the bulk of individual voters is extremely low; second, the number of individuals importantly involved in making authoritative decisions is an extremely small proportion of the total population. These observations may be held to support normative judgments about the nature of democracy. The apathy of the mass, and the maintenance of that apathy, is a desirable feature of the polity on grounds of efficiency. More important, elite rule may be supported on grounds that popular participation, when it does occur, manifests itself as a crudely emotional sense of mutual commitment between authoritarian demogogues and the aroused masses, whose attachment to liberal ideas about individual freedom may be far from complete. Thus elite rule may be thought vital for the effective conduct of democratic business, and for the effective protection of the value of individual freedom.

It is a requirement of this view of the nature of democracy that the ruling elite should share a fundamental consensus on democratic values. It is also important to the protection of liberty that the members of the elite should compete against one another for the offices of public power. Elite rule is not to be confused with permanent government by a clique.

Two imminent dangers are apparent to elite theorists: at one extreme, that the consensus among the elite should degenerate into an undemocratic unanimity, corrupting to both the elite and to society at large; second, at the other extreme, that competition for power among the elements of the elite should become so fierce as to undermine the general coherence of the elite as a whole. In the latter case the elite loses its control over society, and the masses, leaderless, fall prey to the fearful excitements and false promises of fanatics of all varieties.

Accepting the elite view as being accurately descriptive of politics and public administration in Britain, in what ways does the existence of foreign relations affect British democracy? The traditional view of foreign policy as high statecraft is generally highly elitist in its perceptions and judgments. Diplomacy is a subtle business which should be conducted discreetly by those whose training and background qualify them to understand its intricacies and to move easily among the elites of foreign countries. The duty of the foreign policy elite is to defend the existence of democracy at home and further its practical interests abroad. Elite concensus on these two fundamental objectives may be complicated by responsible disagreements, coolly expressed, about exact tactics in dealing with particular issues. Since the foreign elites with which British diplomatists deal may often be distinctly undemocratic in their values and conduct, the proper British attitude to foreign relations must be essentially conservative, placing priority on the maintenance of the British state and the furtherance of its interests, avoiding too close an association with other countries and too close an involvement in their domestic relations. Essentially, the foreign policy elite is committed to democracy at home and to diplomacy abroad, and it does not confuse these two concerns or the two environments to which they refer.

This elite view of foreign policy has been historically repugnant to radical opinion in Britain and has long been attacked along consistent lines. First, it has been contended that a commitment to democracy cannot be morally limited by the frontiers of the state. A regard for individual liberty and dignity is not essentially nationalist but extends to all human beings regardless of their nationality. The foreign policy of a democracy should therefore be informed by democratic values and should be concerned with their defence and propagation wherever practicable. This attitude showed itself most markedly, though not exclusively, in the liberal imperialism which saw the British Empire as a means of spreading democratic values: and this tradition remained evident in the long conflict with the Rhodesian regime over the internal arrangements of authority in Rhodesia. Outside the Empire, the impact of radical opinion on high statecraft was, and is, somewhat less immediate. But it certainly contributed to British support for international organisations such as the League and the UN, and to the British commitment to the idea, if not the exact practices, of an international legal order. Sometimes it encouraged a cautious official support of liberal regimes in foreign countries and, more rarely, support of opposition movements to illiberal regimes. But pressures to direct high foreign policy to these kinds of ends have been, and remain, in conflict with the view that British diplomacy must deal with foreign elites as they are and not as they should be, that the protection and well-being of democracy at home is the proper function of foreign policy, and this function could be impaired, even destroyed, by a commitment to foreign crusades in the cause of democracy.

A second line of attack, particularly prominent in Britain during and after the First World War, concentrates on the harmful effects on citizens of the acceptance of the conception of elitist foreign policy. An elite is prone to act secretly; to enter into deals and alliances with other elites to the detriment of democratic values in third countries; to behave generally as if democracy is inapplicable to foreign policy

F

and thereby to demean democrats, drawing them into costly and even harmful foreign commitments of which they may not approve and about which they may be given little information. The attack on elite foreign policy inspired by this view is four-pronged. It urges the exposure of the foreign policy process to detailed democratic scrutiny and to the authoritative sanction of democratic disapproval. It urges the opening of the ranks of the diplomatic corps to recruits from all social and educational strata. It deplores the tendency of diplomats to move in narrow elitist circles abroad and it is anxious to encourage as many elements of domestic life as possible to be active in foreign concerns and associations. In the international environment it favours the establishment of open international organisations in which international business is conducted in an unsecretive style and from which democrats may hope to see emerge an effective international legal order. It also favours the maximum development of contacts at non-governmental levels between citizens of different nations as a kind of general education in world citizenship.

A third line of attack concentrates on the supposed state-centred values of the foreign policy elite. The effect of elite attitudes which conservatively concentrate on the sanctity of sovereignty is that international conflict is exacerbated, needlessly so in many cases. The concept of the sovereign state is one which compels its adherents to view international life as a struggle. Diplomatists and statesmen of this bent therefore commit themselves to what they see as a kind of war, usually polite in form, with the representatives of other states who share the same attitude. The result for international society as a whole is that the task of tackling common problems (of security, or poverty, or international monetary order) is constantly bedevilled by conflicts between historical entities which have no structural relationship with the basic needs of universal society. Given this viewpoint, the attack on the diplomatic elite is even more fundamental: no less than to displace it from any important role in world affairs. In the place of the foreign policy elite should be put organisations designed to tackle specific problems which assail men of all nationalities, and these organisations should be staffed and operated not by diplomats but by experts in the relevant problems who do not see world problems as a series of issues between sovereign states. In effect, this is a total commitment to transnational organisations as the means of emptying the state and diplomacy of their international standing and, ultimately, of their harmful authority in world society.

An elite view of high statecraft is thus one which has long been the subject of vigorous attack. However, the elite interpretation of democracy is more adaptable than might at first appear, and can even be applied to foreign policy transformed by transnational organisations and transnational systems of social and economic action. Given a transnational governmental environment, the elite may be thought to survive and even to reach its fullest creative potential. It is no longer a national elite narrowly concerned with traditional foreign policy, but the whole elite of democracy, which becomes generally absorbed in the entire range of the complex continuum of domestic–transnational–international politics and public administration. In this conception the democratic elite does not react against other elites but merges with them and becomes, or should become, a truly transnational elite. This elite is shared among the democracies and it develops a common language for dealing with the problems of the democracies. Thus democratic values are served in a setting where states simply constitute one form of public administration. In countries where democracy is a recent structural development its stability and endurance are increased by its incorporation into the political and administrative networks of democracy as a whole. The creation among the democratic countries of a coherent transnational elite has the effect of reducing many of their mutual problems to questions of technical problem-solving, rather than, as formerly, questions of national honour and power conflict. The elitist qualities, of, say, the EEC, are therefore in no way to be deplored. The more that foreign democrats are involved in British government, and *vice versa*, the better for democracy as a whole. The stronger the transnational democratic elite, the less likelihood there is that an undemocratic elite will grow among the Western countries. The elite, being a political fact, needs no justification so long as it serves the conditions in which democratic values prosper.

It is, of course, questionable whether democracy actually works according to the elite model, and it is even more questionable whether it should work in this way. Whether the nature of transnational problems fits the elite model is especially doubtful. For example, efforts to control inflation, which might be argued to be the fundamental problem of the international economy, could hardly be said to resolve themselves into elite decisions on technique, involving as they do almost all sectors of international society. And inflation, in the past, has had some part in the creation of antidemocratic forces, destructive of international order as a whole. Similarly, it might be argued that the interlocking of national democratic elites is irrelevant if the underlying transnational systems to which they address themselves are not truly integrated but fractured by nationalist attitudes among those not included in the grand alliance of elites. The active transformation of foreign policy, it may be argued, is far too fundamental a matter to be left in the hands of elites, actual or imagined.

The pluralist variant

It has long been held that the basic fact of the democratic community is its domination by its constituent groups. From this position, the structure of the democratic system resolves itself, as a matter of observation, into a large number of groups, each of which pursues its interests in a massive field of group pressures. Institutions are included in this field. A government is simply one group among many others. The effectiveness of a government depends on the convergence of group pressures along the lines which it favours. Political parties and the official channels of group communication help to secure this effect, as does the tendency for groups to cancel one another out in the course of their pursuits: groups tend to compete for allocations from limited social resources, and each group therefore tends to create its own opposition. The stability of democracy depends, first, on the existence of a balance between groups, and, second, on the acceptance by groups of the rules of the game as it is played in any particular democracy. If a large group presses its interests intemperately or violently, then in the nature of the case its own opposition, in the form of a contending group or groups, will be motivated to act likewise and to abandon the rules of the game in order to prevent it from acquiring immoderate gains by extreme means. In this way the delicate balance on which democracy depends may be destroyed.

The duties of democratic government, viewed thus, are fourfold. First, it must prevent the balance of democracy from being disturbed by outside forces, military or economic. Second, it must attempt to ensure that social allocations are made in such a way that no major group is motivated to abandon the rules of the game. It clearly assists this activity if total available resources can be increased. Third, having a more general kind of interest than other groups, it must pursue and attempt to regulate these groups in all their concerns, lest in their self-interested tactics they upset the general equilibrium. And, fourth, government must attempt to understand, and meet, the demands of groups which are latent or ill-organised, whose needs might otherwise be neglected in the network of group pressures exerted more expertly and powerfully. A large latent group, a racial minority perhaps, which does not benefit from the rules of the game will eventually cease to be latent and in its newfound coherence is unlikely to show much regard for the rules under which it may feel itself to have suffered, and may thus upset the group equilibrium essential to democracy.

This view of the structure of British society and of the place and duties of government within it carries over into the international arena fairly easily. There need be no essential difference of practice or principle for democratic governments which extend their relations among themselves. In a sense all this does is to add an extra layer of complexity to the group structure of democracy. There is no reason why democratic governments, appreciative of one another's difficulties and limitations, should not conduct themselves rather like any other set of groups, working out another dimension of the rules of the democratic game. Nor is there any sound argument against their developing kinds of governments (a reformed IMF or a stronger EEC, for example) performing functions relating to the maintenance of a democratic balance among themselves.

Again, if it is a function of governments to exercise some vigilance over other groups and interests, it follows that governments must attempt to pursue groups which move strongly in the international environment. The democratic society is an open one, so in a sense groups draw government into their extranational medium of operations. Most obvious examples are multinational companies and banking consortia, which create a group network ignoring national democratic frontiers, yet which may create democratic disequilibrium. Democratic government is obliged to exercise some kind of vigilance over this sort of transnational activity, and in doing so naturally falls into a close set of relations with other democratic governments. Its function in this context is to operate to maintain stability within the group environment as a whole, and this is far from being a national one.

In their interest in increased total wealth, which may be distributed in an equilibriating fashion among contending groups, democratic governments must necessarily be concerned with enlarging markets and exploiting the world's resources in the most effective and least harmful way. This concern with the growth of the international economy must also include a concern with its orderliness. This again draws the democratic government, conceived thus, into intimate association with other governments and gives it an interest in the creation and maintenance of rules of the larger game, played by national governments and transnational groups. The problem of democratic control of traditional high foreign policy in an electoral sense is not a vivid one. The important condition of democracy is the maximum participation of groups of all kinds in a stable transnational systemic environment.

Just as government has an interest in internal affairs, in anticipating and expressing the needs of disadvantaged and poorly organised groups, so at the international level it should have a concern for the requirements of the underdeveloped countries which are unable to make a great practical impact on the group system of the developed world. The more countries which can be inducted into the democratic game, the better for the ultimate security and wellbeing of democracy itself. Countries which are constantly frustrated in their efforts at economic growth are unlikely to show much respect for a method of conducting affairs which has left them alone with their disadvantages. Democratic governments therefore have an interest in opening the Western wealth-creating system to poorer countries in ways which indulge their genuine difficulties.

In the context of a transformed structure of foreign relations, then, the group interpretation of British democracy has much to offer, both analytically and prescriptively. But it is not without defects. To suggest, for example, that government should operate transnationally in order to regulate the activities of transnational groups, should not blind one to the absence of transnational intergovernmental organisations capable of serving this end. It is often argued that there is a transnational governmental interest in regulating tax avoidance and monopoly practices among multinational companies. But no intergovernmental agency exists for this purpose on a geographical scale equivalent to that within which these companies are commonly active. The creation of an appropriate organisation, concerning itself with the detail of domestic, commercial and taxation legislation in a variety of countries, would be no small political undertaking. The central deficiency of the group interpretation of democracy, transposed to the international milieu, is that it tends to ignore the fact that men, including democratic men absorbed in the pursuit of particular group interests, may be inclined to place the national group on a special plane and to equip it with the exceptional quality of sovereignty. To the extent to which international relations conform to the traditional image of an arena of high international statecraft, governments are placed in an entirely different category from other groups, and the relations between them are conditioned by a tender regard for the notion, perhaps entirely misplaced, of the integrity and integration of the national group.

The process variant

Understanding that democracy is variously structured, that it is made up of formal and informal institutions, and that elections and group pressures are essential to the maintenance of democratic values, is not necessarily to acquire much insight into the essential nature of democratic decision. Our final resort, then, is to place ourselves in the position of authoritative democratic policy-makers and to say something about the quality of their actions, when these are properly democratic.

The democratic policy-maker exists in an historical situation. He must to a large extent rely on consent, tacit or explicit, for what he does, and is able to do, among the groups and institutions of his political environment. He is subjected to a host of legitimate pressures, interests and arguments, both national and international, urging him to contrary lines of action. Similarly, in an interdependent environment such as this, a single decision may reverberate and be transformed in all sorts of unforeseen ways. This is a situation in which dogmatism is a dangerous irrelevance. The democratic decision-maker does not assume that the world conforms to an exact set of preconceived notions about it. The world is as it is: massive plans cannot, and should not, be applied to it.

The democratic decision-maker therefore considers alternative policies at the margins of feasible action. He considers conditions likely to result from decisions as small increments to the existing structure of national and international society. He does not chase hellbent after major changes which might upset the measure of justice and order already achieved. Small changes can be achieved, given careful attention to all the interests and powers involved. Even at this low pitch it is impossible to know that what is intended can be attained. But the advantage of incremental decisions is that if they go wrong they can usually be reversed. The statesman does not attempt the immediate creation of, say, an international currency: in association with other democratic statesmen he takes a small step which may lead to further steps in this direction. If the first small step leads, or looks like leading, to unfortunate results he withdraws and considers another small decision. A policy is considered as a marginal change. Large changes are the historical aggregation of a large number of marginal decisions.

A similar approach is extended to values. The democratic policy-maker does not fix his mind on some large value, like liberty or international integration, and then exert himself in some massive effort at its achievement from a premeditated blueprint. He considers whether one small and practicable change adds or detracts from liberty or international integration. He considers what other small changes are possible. And if he has to choose between liberty and international integration, it is only a very small marginal choice that he makes, and it can be readily altered or rescinded at a later stage. Choice between policy alternatives is made on the basis of selection among the marginal changes in social conditions likely to result. Democratic conflicts occur in this context of marginality. Therefore choice is not earthshaking.

This is a rational form of policy-making in a complicated social situation, full of rigidities, where information is necessarily imperfect, where values are open to argument, where civilised social cohesion is set above ideological purity, and where it is impossible to work out all the possible consequences of choice. Action at the margin is likely to be reversible, it is unlikely to transgress well-supported values in any radical way, it is centrally concerned with available means, to which ultimate purposes are always adapted. The democrat has both ends and means in sight, and they are mutually adjustable. Equally, the democratic decision-maker is well adapted to react, incrementally, to fresh inflows of information. He does not close his mind to novel data, nor does he blind himself to the fact that his choices may not have the results he anticipated. He does not delude himself with the idea that he can cure national and international ills, he merely works at them. He has no clear concept of an ideal international society, but he is acutely aware of existing problems, and he attempts to cope with these in a piecemeal way. The democrat operates in a context where power and influence are diffused among a large number of groups—parties, pressure groups, international organisations, other governments. In this structural situation he operates a give-and-take, equilibrium-maintaining, decision-making procedure.

This view of democracy conforms broadly with the British empirical tradition in politics. It concentrates on the pursuit of the practicable. It is disinclined to confront democracy with massive choices of principle. It is not disposed to find earthshaking problems in the changing structure of foreign policy. In a conceptual sense, it is a view which disregards distinctions between the domestic and international settings, between the pursuit of national interests and international interests, between defence and security, between interdependence and economic sovereignty. Conflicts between these goals do not impede the patient investigation of possibilities of resolving policy differences at the margins of adjustment. The democrat proceeds by dealing incrementally with the application of values to problems. He operates in this way domestically; and he does exactly the same in the company of foreign democrats. Because he operates thus, the element of discordance in his values (between national and international loyalties perhaps) is not raised to an unbearable level of tension. In the pursuit of the applicable and the practicable these problems are contained by politics.

There are three basic criticisms of this view of democracy. First, the patient adjuster, as a matter of fact, may tend to adjust more to the stronger pressures brought to bear upon him, and may thus ignore the silent and the weak, both nationally and internationally. He lives in a world of powers. As a moral recommendation this view of democracy is therefore less than inspiring. Second, mutual adjustment may work adequately among democrats, but it is a characteristic of the international milieu that it contains large numbers of highly undemocratic governments. Adjusting to the demands of these governments could easily slip into a policy of appeasement. In this kind of situation massive issues of principle may occur all too readily and there may be no substitute for old-fashioned military strength and a blunt refusal to give way. Third, changes wrought by mutual adjustment among democratic representatives at the transnational and international levels may not be marginal. Political marginality is a highly subjective quality. Sectors of opinion in Britain have been alarmed by constitutional departures stemming from British entry to the European Community. In establishing settings within which mutual adjustment may be practised, democrats may thus agree to transformations which, to other democrats, appear to be distinctly non-incremental.

CONCLUSION

The existence of traditional foreign policy and diplomacy has always constituted a problem for British democracy. The transformation of foreign policy, resulting from the transnational blurring of the distinction between domestic and external politics and government, creates some new problems. Viewed from the standpoint of the maintenance of democracy itself, rather from the viewpoint of the exact maintenance of a particular national system of democracy, these new problems are in no way inherently intractable. Indeed the six views of the nature of democracy discussed here were all readily adapted to fit the requirements of the changing structure of British foreign policy and to offer prescriptive suggestions relevant to this shifting milieu.

9 Control

Let us again start from the view that the foreign policy of Britain is the external strategy and actions of the state. The control and direction of foreign policy in this sense is embedded in the traditional apparatus of the state. The British external affairs ministry, the Foreign and Commonwealth Office, provides the channels through which the state acts abroad. It also interprets the international environment for the government and advises on the merits of alternative courses of action. The armed forces, controlled through the Ministry of Defence, provide the strength which substantiates foreign policy. The Cabinet, suitably equipped with committees such as its Defence and Oversea Policy Committee, formulates the will of the government in external relations, considers and coordinates the internal requirements of chosen foreign policies, supervises the domestic fulfilment of external obligations. The government, principally in the persons of the Prime Minister and Foreign Secretary, makes known in general terms, the range and reasoning of its foreign policy in the British assembly, the House of Commons. There the people's deputies, constituting the forum of the nation, debate the grand strategy of British foreign policy; from their views, and from the interplay of government and assembly, emerges the general will of the sovereign people on the state's course in international seas. Thus the ship of state is navigated.

This high vision of foreign policy has been assailed by a large number of secular changes. The external affairs ministry, the Foreign and Commonwealth Office, has felt their force most particularly. The conception of the duty of this ministry as one of generalist concern with all Britain's foreign connections, with all foreigners that is, is one which has been shaken by political facts and administrative doctrine. The idea of a public servant as a general administrator, skilled in operating the mechanisms of public affairs as a whole, does not prosper in a period when governments become increasingly involved in the detail of highly technical systems in industry, finance and the social services. Similarly, the idea that any ministry should deal with a specific body of people, foreigners in the case of the Foreign and Commonwealth Office, in all their activities, has long been held to militate against clear and effective perceptions of the complex functions of government as they impinge on specific aspects of the social system. In its generality the traditional conception of the foreign ministry thus contradicts recent trends of thought and practice in public administration.

In the external environment the Foreign and Commonwealth Office is confronted by a vastly increased area of operations. The emancipation of all sorts of colonies has proliferated states on an unexampled scale. Keeping the British government informed on political conditions in all the states of its international setting is clearly an impossible task. Domestic bureaucracry might be able to deal with the massive quantity of paper generated, but no minister or cabinet could possibly absorb the information contained in it. Nor need they. Britain's relations with a large number of states are tenuous and the ability of British governments to intervene in internal political affairs is negligible, as is their capacity to circumscribe further the already slight capabilities for foreign action of many small countries. In a sense Britain keeps a diplomatic apparatus in many states in case of an unforeseeable emergency, and when the emergency occurs a British government is likely to be unable to make a distinctive and effective response to it. As a department dealing with foreigners the FCO is thus confronted by an enlarged field of operations in much of which it is powerless to operate.

Its unspecialised nature is exposed by a further change in the international milieu, which is the appearance within it of a large number of specialised organisations. Many of these lie outside the competence of official diplomatic involvement in the sense that they are private gatherings of scientists, businessmen and suchlike. As well, a number of powerful non-governmental domestic organisations, like the TUC and the CBI, are quite capable of conducting their own foreign relations with equivalent overseas bodies and with international organisations, official and private. The expert nature of many intergovernmental organisations also undermines the status of traditional diplomacy. There is little that a traditional diplomatist can add to the work of the Organisation for Economic Cooperation and Development: in an organisation such as this the principal task of a diplomatic mission is to facilitate visits by domestic experts from, or sponsored by, a range of home ministries. This general trend has shown itself particularly in the relations of Britain and the other Western developed countries. The number of government departments which may wish to conduct relatively low-level negotiations, or to exchange technical information, with other departments in Western European countries is virtually equivalent to the number of ministries which actually exist at any given time. This intense international activity in almost all branches of public administration means that a British mission in such a country becomes a miniature version of the whole apparatus of Whitehall, to which traditional diplomacy as such contributes little. Moreover, the style in which governments conduct their relations at the highest level has changed. For some time the practice of governments has not conformed to high diplomatic doctrine. The Western governments conduct their extremely sensitive economic relations in a fairly direct fashion, which impinges little on the work of foreign ministries. Meetings among central bankers are not the responsibility of foreign ministers, and the British Chancellor of the Exchequer usually maintains fairly close direct, and sometimes very personal, contacts with his fellow economic ministers in the Western community. Prime ministers have also shown a marked tendency to depart into the external environment to cultivate their colleagues. The central characteristics of this kind of development are, first, its commonplace frequency, and, second, its extensive range over the functions and membership of a government. Each major department is its own foreign ministry. The more that practices such as these transform high policy, the more complex and intimate become direct contacts between governments, the less relevant is the conception of a diplomatic corps as the expression and interpreter of the state's external strategy.

Another change has been worked on high foreign policy by the depth and breadth of alliance relations. Britain's most important alliances no longer take the simple form of treaty obligations supplemented, perhaps, by occasional staff talks at the military level. The treaty organisations of the Western alliance have a complexity which demands daily governmental attention. This is not simply a technical concern. Most of what remains of high British policy, towards Eastern Europe, say, or towards arms control in Europe, is essentially alliance policy. High policy which is at root alliance policy develops characteristics dissimilar from those of traditional statecraft. Intra-alliance politics can be exceedingly detailed and wide ranging. The penchant of American governments for linking military questions with questions relating to the regulation of the Western economy, for example, draws matters of economic technicality, not a traditional concern of diplomatists, into an apparent field of high policy.

If the British external affairs ministry were to be able to maintain the legitimacy of the notion that it controls the channels of Britain's foreign relations and is the primary source of advice on policies impinging on the international arena, then it would clearly become by far the most powerful of government departments. It would regulate the whole of Britain's relations in the European Community and would thus become a force to be reckoned with in, say, decisions affecting investment plans in the nationalised industries. No such effect is likely. But if the mass of diplomatic reporting is judged to be of indifferent significance to the situation in which Britain finds itself, and no specialist functions are deemed appropriate to diplomatists, it follows that the primary duty of the foreign affairs ministry is simply to service, when required, other departments in the conduct of their own foreign relations.

The adaptation of diplomacy to these new circumstances can be approached in two ways. First, the foreign affairs ministry can be drastically pruned. In fact, since 1965 the British diplomatic service has been steadily contracting, and is likely to continue to do so for the next decade. An indiscriminate reduction could be harmful to the range of British contacts with Western developed countries, so a case has been made (notably in the 'Duncan Report' of 1969, Cmnd 4107) that in the 'Outer Area' where British external contacts are few, missions could be reduced to the basic strength of, say, three officers, supplemented temporarily from the FCO and other missions as occasion demands.

A second course is to discover a functional speciality for the diplomatic service comparable with the functional nature of much of the administrative work of the 'home' civil service. The suggestion most often made in this connection (and developed again in the 'Duncan Report') is that the commercial work of British overseas missions should be increased. From this viewpoint, the most constantly important factor in British external relations is British trade, and this has commonly failed to expand at a satisfactory rate. By furthering the foreign commercial activities of British exporters, the diplomatist contributes to the growth of the British economy and thereby to the status and influence of Britain abroad. Thus a major function of the diplomatist should be to provide a market research facility for British traders, to provide direct services to travelling British businessmen in the form of contacts and appointments, and to collect and digest, particularly in Western Europe, information on local regulations relating to property acquisition, insurance and suchlike. British diplomatists should also be aware of the investment needs, and the opportunuties, of the development areas in Britain and should exert themselves to interest foreigners accordingly.

A number of problems attach to giving this kind of economic function to diplomacy. It is already a matter of wide comment that British embassies probably provide commercial services on a scale greater than those of other comparable European countries. Generally, European chambers of commerce and trading associations perform many of the services which British diplomacy has undertaken. In the long run it is not entirely unlikely that British businessmen may prefer to work through their own organisations, particularly in the Community. If this happens, a further blow will be struck at the place of diplomacy in foreign relations. The most important export decisions of British companies are made in their respective boardrooms and there is no evidence to suggest that the FCO is granted access to these. So the provision of 'low' services is not to be equated with great influence on low policies. And large multinational companies are well placed to provide their own international services: this is one of the reasons why they come into existence. They have no particular need for official diplomacy. This is especially so in the case of international banks and banking consortia. The greater the integration of the Western economy, the greater is likely to be the role of transnational companies, which need not all be on a massive scale. Diplomatic services to private industry and commerce may thus become rapidly redundant because of the growth of private industrial and commercial transnationalism. Similarly, the tendency of the Foreign Office to impinge on the functions of other major ministries, notably departments of trade and industry, does nothing to increase the importance of diplomacy. There can be no prospect of the FCO taking over the roles of domestic departments, if only because of its inexpert nature. To the degree to which it merely services them it again reduces itself as an organ of policy-making and execution in external dimensions, while adding, one suspects, to the intricacy of the Whitehall apparatus of interdepartmental coordination.

If diplomacy is the main instrument of traditional foreign policy, then the Cabinet is the director of its grand strategy, orchestrating the strength and interests of Britain to maintain a forceful, distinctive and consistent presence in the international arena. The primary qualification of this exalted image of the Cabinet must spring from the contemplation of the external setting of British governments and of their reduced standing in it. Traditionally, the field of foreign relations is not a legislative one for its components, it is a milieu in which governments exercise power and influence over one another. If follows that the more Britain declines in terms of power and influence, the less foreign policy a British Cabinet can make, because the less notice foreign governments will take of Britain. If Britain ceases to be capable of projecting an effective foreign policy, the foreign policy role of the Cabinet becomes correspondingly less significant.

This conclusion, which is founded on the traditional conception of the nature of foreign policy, misses much of the subtlety of Britain's international situation. It must be true that the discontinuities of the international arena, notably that between the first-rank powers and others, have circumscribed traditional British foreign policy. But they have not circumscribed Britain's foreign relations. The reverse has been the case. The connections between Britain and the rest of the Western community, particularly the European part of it, have developed vastly and, one may think, will continue to do so.

In a sense high foreign policy has survived, but it has become a kind of international community effort. European relations with the United States, long regarded as the singular prerogative of British foreign policy, have tended to become a communal concern of the European governments. Similarly, relations with the Soviet Union in the context of European security and arms control have largely become a matter in which the Western European governments must move as a whole. To a small and imperfect degree this is a matter of fact. One might also urge that it should become a matter of ordinary political prudence. When one of the first-rank powers concentrates on a bilateral relationship with a lesser government, such as that of Britain, it must tend to play on the latter's circumscribed capabilities. Traditional sovereign foreign policy must in these circumstances be an exposure of the weaknesses of the second-class European governments. There is thus a motivation for Community governments wishing to operate a high foreign policy to do so in a communal fashion. This motivation manifests itself in regular gatherings of Western European foreign ministers and heads of government. To the degree to which this approach works, it makes high foreign policy a slow and laborious business. Taken very far, it would transform foreign policy in the sense that the actual foreign policy-making process would itself become a Community matter. The British

Cabinet would become an item in a larger machine producing a kind of European high foreign policy. The resulting strategies would therefore not be peculilarly British in the traditional sense. In a small way, this kind of change can already be seen to have taken place. There can be little doubt, for instance, that British attitudes towards the charges demanded by the government of Malta for the military facilities of the island have not represented a specifically British policy but have been an amalgam of alliance needs and conditions in the Mediterranean.

The second kind of transformation of British foreign policy, on which this essay has repeatedly dwelt, lies in the extension of the range of Britain's transnational official relations. The more that ordinary domestic policies are affected by foreign influences, the more does the foreign dimension become an ordinary part of British public administration. Given this kind of transformation, the conception of the British Cabinet as a body coordinating the resources of the British political system behind a specific foreign policy strategy is anachronistic. The problem of coordination becomes the far more intricate one of coordinating British governmental concerns in a particular domestic area with forms of governmental activity in that same area in the transnational setting. In this way coordination has become a far more subtle business than formerly; and the notion of the British Cabinet as the supreme coordinating body loses much of its force when the coordination in question is not specifically national coordination but the coordination of governmental functions within transnational systems.

Turning to the third mechanism of domestic control, there has long been discontent among British democrats with the powers of the House of Commons in the direction of high foreign policy. This assembly debates, and may approve or otherwise, the more important treaties to which the government has put its signature. It questions the two members of the government formally most responsible for high policy, the Prime Minister and the Foreign Secretary, given that the latter is a member of the Commons. It conducts general debates, relating to the Queen's Speech for example, which range widely through all aspects of international relations and British foreign policy. And, from time to time, it is mustered to discuss specific foreign policy issues as matters of urgent public interest.

As the forum of the nation, and the rack of the executive, the House of Commons is often held to be substantially impotent in matters of high foreign policy. Skilled parliamentarians, which the Prime Minister and Foreign Secretary should be, need reveal little to Commons

F*

questioners. Additionally, given that the modes of high diplomacy are extremely discreet if not entirely secret, it is extremely difficult for ordinary members to phrase precise questions. In the matter of traditional treaties, the Commons tends to be confronted with what may represent an important public commitment in a cut-and-dried form. In the nature of the case, a government cannot allow an agreed treaty to be amended. The only scope for amendment lies where enabling legislation is required. But given the nature of traditional treaties, this is seldom necessary. Similarly, in debates on foreign policy as specific matters of pointed public concern, a government which is contemplating an important overseas action is unlikely to want to publicise its plans, because it would thereby forewarn its international enemies. It cannot therefore expose itself fully to public debate in the Commons. And when some international action is under way the Commons is further inhibited by two considerations: first, that a scheme once started develops its own impetus, and, anyway, can hardly be discussed in terms of success or failure while in progress, particularly when success or failure may seem to be related to what is said in the House of Commons; second, that once a British commitment is made, particularly if troops are involved, a sense of national solidarity and duty may intervene to the detriment of high policy debate.

For reasons such as these, it has been a repeated suggestion, even among subscribers to the high doctrine of foreign policy, that the House of Commons should be equipped with a specialised committee on foreign affairs able to examine the minutiae of government policies and actions in the international arena. Such a reform has been resisted by governments of all complexions on two fundamental grounds. First, it would work to the detriment of British interests were the nature of Britain's negotiating positions to become known before or during the course of negotiations, since foreign governments could adapt their strategies accordingly. Second, such a committee would follow too closely the work of a single department, the foreign affairs ministry, and would thereby radically undermine the ministerial responsibility of the Foreign Secretary in two ways: foreign governments would be placed in a position of not quite knowing whether they were negotiating with a government minister or with an assembly committee; second, the House of Commons as a whole might itself be unable to pin responsibility for a policy on a minister, or upon a government, if one of its own committees was simultaneously active and effective in the very same matter.

If the high foreign policy role of the House of Commons has long been felt to be incomplete, the decline of high foreign policy may be argued to have rendered it irrelevant. Specifically British foreign policy now rarely yields treaties in the grand manner. Grand treaties are more likely to be the product of alliance policies if they involve Britain at all. Any future treaties relating to European security are likely to be approached in this way. The relevance of grand national debate to the long and detailed evolution of alliance policy is clearly questionable. Moreover, the decline of her strength renders the circumstances of Britain so compelling that there is a large measure of high foreign policy continuity between British governments. Great issues can constantly be found in British policy, continued membership of Nato is one, and dissent can be expressed in these high terms in the House of Commons. But when an opposition becomes a government it finds itself continuing substantially along established lines. The great issue turns out not to be an issue at all. Britain's decline also means that many of the issues which excite public disquiet—the problems of Vietnam have often fallen into this category—are issues which British governments do not have the capability to influence. In these circumstances, an emphasis on grand debates in the Commons may be equated with an emphasis on high rhetoric empty of all practical effect.

Arguments such as these are by no means unassailable, and they will be taken up at a later stage. For the present, it is appropriate to query whether the House of Commons does see both itself and foreign affairs in entirely grand outlines. There is certainly a body of opinion which would hold that the British assembly has functions which do not fall within the terms of such a conception. The House of Commons should, it is contended, acquaint itself with the details of public affairs, both to inform itself and the electorate. It should not merely criticise but also advise governments. It should provide the essential mechanism of stable rule in a democracy by providing channels whereby the people's representatives enter, both critically and otherwise, into the process of government, thereby conferring on it the democratic consent of an active society. An assembly conceived in this way must enter closely in foreign affairs in two senses: first, its intervention in domestic government must necessarily run into the external environment because so much of what government does, and can do, relates to what is being done in transnational, particularly Community, dimensions; second, if it is the duty of the House of Commons to enter into government wherever government takes place, then its members must, and in some

measure do, make themselves effective in international assemblies, such
as those of the Community and the North Atlantic Treaty Organisation.

The transnational transformation of foreign policy has had two
apparently contrasting effects on the British assembly conceived as a
participant in government. First, the Commons in its committee in-
vestigations into government, naturally moves outside the territory of
the United Kingdom. A Trade and Industry Subcommittee of the
Public Expenditure Committee has thus conducted proceedings in
Brussels, taking evidence from members of the European Commission on
questions relating to regional policy. Second, the legislative authority
of the Commons, which is seldom held to be outstanding, may seem to
be further curtailed by the legislative powers of institutions, centrally
those of the Community, acting transnationally. But this latter effect
may turn out to be more apparent than real. Given that the Community
is a slow-moving and not markedly secretive body, the more emphasis
that is given to the Commons as a participant in government and the
more active its members are in the European Assembly, the greater may
be the involvement of British parliamentarians in what would formerly have been considered external affairs. The existing principle that
ministers should inform the Commons well in advance of proposed
regulations before they are approved by the European Council of
Ministers, thus giving members the opportunity to table detailed
questions and to ask for adjournment debates before the imposition
of transnational rules, is entirely secondary to the future of more
fundamental changes in the attitude of the House of Commons to the
place of its members in the process of government wherever it occurs.
Along these lines it is possible to press the case that the House of Commons has lost no standing in international relations. The less high foreign
policy there is, the less significant is the longstanding deficiency of the
Commons as a mechanism controlling its course. The greater the
transnational element in government, and the more the Commons
regards itself as a legitimate and necessary participant in the whole process of government, the more impact does this assembly and its members have on the detail of Britain's foreign relations.

OLD ROLES AND NEW SETTINGS

Though the transformation of high foreign policy creates complicated
problems, and opportunities, for the domestic institutions of control,
their old roles have not disappeared and they are not necessarily irrele-

vant to the new milieu. However one cares to view the international setting's potentialities, it remains currently the case that within it the primary centres of authority are national governments. Within the Western association many of the actions of governments affect other governments. It can therefore be argued that this association requires more diplomacy not less, because each government must be able to speak directly and discreetly to the others, and, through the political reporting of its diplomatists, must know what political constraints and impulses play on other governments. Where decisions of governments are most likely to be interdependent, diplomacy should increase its efforts to maintain the flow and political relevance of intergovernmental communications.

Nor is this traditional kind of diplomatic role obliterated by notions of systemic integration. However many transnational systems one may perceive, it remains broadly the case that Western governments are held electorally responsible for the course of public events at their domestic political levels. This may not be entirely reasonable or fair, since transnational systems produce effects which national governments may have difficulty in coping with to the satisfaction of their supporters. But while this tendency of national politics persists, not only will some politicians in their toils be prone to denounce foreign devils but national governments, concerned with electoral survival, will be generally anxious to establish a coherent and perhaps forceful image of themselves as international actors. Though there may be an element of charade in this kind of display, it must be the case that for practical political reasons national governments, unconcerned for the most part with metaphysical flights about state sovereignty, will remain exceedingly sensitive creatures. The need for an appropriately sensitive means of diplomatic communication between them is therefore, one might argue, enhanced by interdependence and integration, which widens the area of their vulnerability to foreign slights and misfortunes, real or imagined.

The necessity for traditional diplomacy might be reduced were major political parties to become intimately linked at, say, a Community level. Why should not a leading German Social Democrat become a minister in a British Labour Cabinet? And one can think of several eminent Frenchmen who might make admirable foreign ministers in British Conservative governments. Visions such as these, in an age which is still struggling through the outer mists of romantic nationalism, are sadly unrealistic. At a very mundane level, British political parties have hardly been at the forefront of efforts to build interparty links at the European level. Anyway, however strong such links might be, while democratic government is dominated by national elections governments in different countries are likely to be of different party complexions, and the need for diplomacy to operate between them in these circumstances is substantially undiminished.

Moreover, the growth of transnational and international organisations in the affairs of the second-class governments does not replace diplomacy by something entirely novel. The grouping together of European elements within Nato, for example, raises the most delicate questions of policy and diplomacy. How far should the coherence of this group be taken? What sort of relationship should be built with an undemocratic government such as that of Greece? How is France to be accommodated? The place of diplomacy in investigating the political implications of specialised organisations, and in providing some of the skills to make them work, is not an inconsiderable one.

Similarly, it may be contended that while the British Cabinet remains the focus of British politics it cannot be absolved from responsibility for foreign policy. The degree to which it enters into the discrete processes of transnational systemic control is irrelevant to its central foreign policy role, since what it does is transformed into a series of high policy decisions by the fact that it is subjected to the vigilant concern of domestic politics. And while the British party system remains roughly as it is, the practice of Cabinet collective responsibility for all decisions of the executive is likely to remain an active principle of British politics, compelling governments to move into the transnational environment backwards, always attentive to considerations of domestic party unity and sensitive to the pressures of the least internationally minded of their members. Nor is it entirely an operational reality that traditional problems of high policy have ceased to assail British governments. The questions relating to the future of the British nuclear force may not be questions of mighty universal importance, but they are still questions of high policy for a second-class power. The fact that British actions have diminished in their external impact does not necessarily transform them qualitatively. The question of British arms exports to South Africa could very well be argued to be one of negligible importance, since whichever way the decision goes its impact on international security and upon internal South African politics is negligible. This may be true. But such an issue raises strategic and political questions of the highest kind. To argue that the issue is an unimportant one because of the reduced power of Britain is an act of moral surrender. The quality of a problem is not changed by the relatively minor effects of any decision relating to it. While issues of this kind occur, the British Cabinet remains an organ of high policy, albeit on a diminished scale.

It remains the case that Britain still finds herself, from time to time, in direct conflict with another state in matters of clashing and highly specific foreign policy interests. While a very small country such as Iceland can don the raiment of state sovereignty and attempt to assert the imperatives of state necessity in the international arena in a way which appears to be directly harmful to specific British interests, then British governments will be expected to maintain, in a reserved way perhaps, a similar role. Issues such as those which have brought Britain and Iceland into conflict may not be matters of massive security risk to the world at large, and perhaps they are best settled in a multilateral way. But they remain issues of high policy from the classical mould.

Connecting the House of Commons and its membership with transnational organisations and assemblies in the pursuit of detailed involvement in the functions of government as these affect the British populace, is not an entirely revolutionary process. True, the conception of the House of Commons as the forum of the nation, the expression of the will of the State, seems somewhat incongruously heroic in an age of increasing technicality in government and international affairs. It nevertheless remains, one might argue, a relevant and desirable conception for two reasons. First, as suggested above, individual issues of high policy still occur, diminished in scale though they may be. When they do occur there is every reason why the Commons should act in the grand manner. Second, British integration into larger systems may be seen as resulting from past decisions and policies of high statecraft. Membership of Nato and the Community are examples. In a sense these decisions must be continually renewed while Britain remains capable of abandoning such organisations. While this element of national consent remains a prominent aspect of Britain's international involvements, claims of parliamentary sovereignty are real enough. That the British assembly should actively question and renew British consent to international attachments is both inevitable and necessary to the continuance of consent itself. The grand approach to international affairs on the part of the assembly is a certain consequence of the fact that international connections, both in Europe and elsewhere, fall far short of what might be accurately described as federal. Given this to be so, the idea if not the daily practice of sovereignty is likely to be cherished, if only to ensure that in the event of the Community acquiring an undemocratic set of governments, the British could withdraw to their island swiftly and cleanly, accepting the consequences with moral self-confidence.

CONCLUSION

The changing structure of British foreign policy renders the control of Britain's external relations a far more various and complex matter than formerly. This increasing complexity does not make redundant any of the traditional instruments of control. In some senses their importance and effectiveness is increased. But by placing them in a situation where they are confronted with issues which conform to the high image of foreign policy and with issues which conform to the image of an open society in which government itself is partly a transnational process, it multiplies the parameters within which they operate and requires them to perform different kinds of roles at the same time.

10 The changing structure of British foreign policy

The methodology of this essay has been straightforward. We started by setting out an orthodox definition of the nature of foreign policy. We then examined the assumptions of this orthodoxy and found grounds for believing them to be mistaken. The possibility that foreign policy itself might undergo a structural transformation through a complicated merging of the national entity into transnational systems, led us to reverse the usual procedure of foreign policy analysis. Instead of examining the historical record of the foreign actions and dispositions of British governments, we attempted to outline some of the problems and potentialities, harmful and otherwise, of the milieu of which Britain forms a part. This led to an examination of the possible paths which British governments might take within this milieu. This examination drew us to emphasise the pressures on British governments to proceed further into transnational enterprises in the task of rendering governable the fields of stress to which British society is subjected. Accepting this process as a real and continuing one, we then considered how best to understand the present and future impact of such developments upon British power, British democracy and upon the traditional instruments for the formulation and control of British foreign policy.

This simple methodology does not lead to simple conclusions. This is to be expected for two reasons. First, though stressing the structural changes which British foreign policy is undergoing, we have not propounded a coherent doctrine of the future shape of international society. Change has not been conceived as a process of movement from a clearly understood past to an equally clear, but radically different, model of the future. Second, it has not been suggested that foreign policy structures and conceptions of the past are being obliterated. So, while accepting the process of transformation, we have also repeatedly referred to the problems of foreign policy and international politics in the context of an environment of sovereign states exerting power and influence over one another in the pursuit of their national interests. We have taken one model, the traditional structural model of foreign policy, and we have set against it not another model but an attitude which is not bound by the supposed imperatives of statehood and which sees no reason why the existence of national governments should preclude the existence of order and government within transnational systems. Indeed, this is an attitude which sees the requisites of national and transnational government as profoundly interdependent, and it leads us to treat British problems in a generalised way. This is a necessary consequence of perceiving foreign policy not as one set of problems relating to the state's external environment, but as complicated and related sets of problems created by systems within international society, which are therefore both internal and external for a national community such as Britain's. Existing foreign policy is not compared with past foreign policy and with a conception of future foreign policy; it is seen as a congeries of concerns and involvements containing intimations of the end of British foreign policy itself. The problems of foreign policy both reflect and require the transformation of foreign policy. These problems are created by the pursuit of policy objectives, such as safety through security, which can be achieved only through participation in transnational organisations having some measure of direct control over British resources. They are also intrinsic to the pursuit of international objectives, such as order in the Western international economy and humanity in its treatment of the poor, which presuppose a sustained measure of Community integration and a readiness to enmesh the Community with other transnational institutions. Remaining responsibly active in large concerns in world society requires the British to be active in the development and creation of transnational organisations.

But the transformation of traditional foreign policy is not wholly a matter of political objectives and strategies. It is also a matter of intellectual and moral commitment. For there is nothing inevitable about this transformation. As we have seen, it is threatened in two general ways. First, transnationalism has been markedly linked in the past with American foreign policy and with the limited international order largely created by the United States. A narrowing of American policies would place the responsibility for the maintenance of the impetus of change on other governments. Yet in the past many lesser Western governments, particularly those of Britain, have tended to wait for, and respond to, initiatives from the United States. Second, the structures of national sovereignty and traditional foreign policy, and the political language of national solidarity in a hostile world, are still in active existence. It has been argued in this essay that there is no necessary conflict between transnationalism and the structures, powers and values of national politics and government. Yet the concepts and practices of national and transnational complementarity are complex and may seem to threaten the psychological security provided by simple illusions of national autonomy and sovereignty.

Further reading

Because of the nature of this essay, which is both introductory and discursive, the text has not been burdened with footnotes. In the following list some items are marked by a star. These are the works to which the writer is most aware of his indebtedness, which is complete and unrepayable.

ARON, R. *Peace and War*, Weidenfeld & Nicolson, 1966.

BACHRACH, P. *The Theory of Democratic Elitism*, University of London Press, 1969.

BARKER, E. *Britain in a Divided Europe*, Weidenfeld & Nicolson, 1971.

BEARD, C. *The Idea of the National Interest*, Macmillan, 1934.

*BEATON, L. *The Reform of Power*, Chatto & Windus, 1972.

BEHRMAN, J. *National Interests and the Multinational Enterprise*, Prentice-Hall, 1970.

BELL, C. *Negotiation from Strength*, Chatto & Windus, 1962.

BELL, C. *The Conventions of Crisis*, Oxford University Press, 1971.

*BELOFF, M. *New Dimensions in Foreign Policy*, Allen & Unwin, 1961.

BELOFF, M. 'International integration and the modern state', in *Journal of Common Market Studies*, ii, 1963, 52–62.

BELOFF, M. *The Future of British Foreign Policy*, Secker & Warburg, 1969.

*BOARDMAN, R. and GROOM, A., eds. *The Management of Britain's External Relations*, Macmillan, 1973.

BRAYBROOKE, D. and LINDBLOM, C. *A Strategy of Decision*, Free Press, Glencoe, 1963.

BRENNER, M. *Technocratic Politics and the Functional Theory of European Integration*, Cornell University Press, 1969.

BROWN, N. *European Security 1972–1980*, London, Royal United Services Institute for Defence Studies, 1972.

BUCHAN, A., ed. *Europe's Futures, Europe's Choices*, Chatto & Windus, 1969.

*BURROWS, B. and IRWIN, C. *The Security of Western Europe*, London, Knight, 1972.

CAMPS, M. *Britain and the European Community 1955–1963*, Princeton University Press, 1964.

CARR, E. H. *The Twenty Years' Crisis, 1919–1939: an introduction to the study of international relations*, Macmillan, 1939.

CHARLESWORTH, J. *Contemporary Political Analysis*, Collier-Macmillan, 1967.

CLARKE, W. and PULAY, G. *The World's Money*, Allen & Unwin, 1970.

CLAUDE, I. *Swords into Ploughshares*, University of London Press, 1965.

CLENDENNING, E. *The Euro-Dollar Market*, Oxford University Press, 1970.

*CLEVELAND, H. *The Atlantic Idea and Its European Rivals*, McGraw-Hill, 1966.

COMMITTEE on REPRESENTATIONAL SERVICES OVERSEAS, 1962–63, *Report* (Chairman: Lord Plowden), Cmnd 2276, HMSO, 1964.

COOMBES, D. *Politics and Bureaucracy in the European Community*, Allen & Unwin, London, 1970.

*COOPER, R. *The Economics of Interdependence*, McGraw-Hill, 1968.

COOPER, R. *Sterling, European Monetary Unification, and the International Monetary System*, London, British-North American Committee, 1972.

*COOPER, R. 'Economic interdependence and foreign policy in the 'seventies', *World Politics*, xxiv, no. 2, 1972, 159–81.

DAHL, R. *Preface to Democratic Theory*, University of Chicago Press, 1956.

EASTON, D. *A Framework for Political Analysis*, Prentice-Hall, 1965.

EASTON. D, *A Systems Analysis of Political Life*, Wiley, 1965.

ETZIONI, A. *Political Unification*, Holt, Rinehart & Winston, 1965.

ETZIONI, A. *The Active Society*, Collier-Macmillan, 1968.

EULAU, H., ELDERSVELD, S. and JANOWITZ, M. eds. *Political Behaviour*, Free Press, Glencoe, 1960.

FOREIGN and COMMONWEALTH REVIEW COMMITTEE on OVERSEAS REPRESENTATION, 1968–69, *Report* (Chairman: Sir Val Duncan), Cmnd 5107, HMSO, 1969.

FRANKEL, J. *The Making of Foreign Policy*, Oxford University Press, 1963.

GALTUNG, J. 'A structural theory of integration', *Journal of Peace Research*, v, 1968, 75–95.

*GILPIN, R. 'The politics of transnational economic relations', *International Organisation*, xxv, 1971, 398–419

GROSS, F. *Foreign Policy Analysis*, New York, Philosophical Library, 1954.

HAAS, E. *Beyond the Nation-State*, Stanford University Press, 1964.

HAWTREY, R. *Economic Aspects of Sovereignty*, Longman, 1952.

HAYEK, F. *The Constitution of Liberty*, Routledge & Kegan Paul, 1960.

HILSMAN, R. and GOOD, R., eds. *Foreign Policy in the 'Sixties*, Johns Hopkins Press, 1965.

HOFFMANN, S. *Gulliver's Troubles, Or the Setting of American Foreign Policy*, McGraw-Hill, 1968.

*HUNTINGTON, S. H. 'Transnational organizations in world politics', *World Politics*, xxv, no. 3, April 1973, 333–68.

*KAISER, K. and MORGAN, R., eds. *Britain and West Germany: changing societies and the future of foreign policy*, Oxford University Press, 1971.

KAPLAN, M. *System and Process in International Politics*, Wiley, 1957.

*KEOHANE, R. O. and NYE, J. S., eds. *Transnational Relations in World Politics*, Harvard University Press, 1971.

*KINDLEBERGER, C. *Power and Money*, Macmillan, 1970.

KINDELBERGER, C., ed. *The International Corporation*, Massachusetts Institute of Technology, 1970.

KINDLEBERGER, C. and SHONFIELD, A., eds. *North American and Western European Economic Policies*, Macmillan, 1971.

KNORR, K. *The War Potential of Nations*, Princeton University Press, 1956.

KNORR, K. *On the Uses of Military Power in the Nuclear Age*, Princeton University Press, 1966.

KNORR, K. and ROSENAU, J., eds. *Contending Approaches to International Politics*, Princeton University Press, 1969.

KNORR, K. and VERBA, S., eds. *The International System: Theoretical Essays*, Princeton University Press, 1961.

LACQUEUR, W. *Europe Since Hitler*, Weidenfeld & Nicolson, 1970.

*LEIFER, M., ed. *Constraints and Adjustments in British Foreign Policy*, Allen & Unwin, 1972.

LERNER, D. and LASSWELL, H. *The Policy Sciences*, Stanford University Press, 1951.

LINDBLOM, C. E. *The Intelligence of Democracy*, Collier-Macmillan, 1965.

LINDBLOM, C. E. *The Policy-Making Process*, Prentice-Hall, 1965.

LOVELL, J. *Foreign Policy in Perspective*, Holt, Rinehart & Winston, 1970.

LUARD, E., ed. *The Evolution of International Organisations*, Thames & Hudson, 1966.

LUARD, E. *Conflict and Peace*, University of London Press, 1970.

MACHLUP, F. *International Payments, Debts and Gold*, Scribners, 1964.

MCCLELLAND, C. A. *Theory and the International System*, Collier-Macmillan, 1966

MACRIDIS, R., ed. *Foreign Policy in World Politics*, Prentice-Hall, 1967.

MANSER, W. A. *Britain in Balance*, Longman, 1971.

MAYO, H. *An Introduction to Democratic Theory*, Oxford University Press, 1960.

*MITRANY, D. *A Working Peace System*, Oxford University Press, 1943.

*MODELSKI, G. *A Theory of Foreign Policy*, Praeger, 1962.

MODELSKI, G. *Principles of World Politics*, Collier-Macmillan, 1972.

MORGAN, R. *West European Politics Since 1945*, Batsford, 1973.

MORGENTHAU, H. *In Defence of the National Interest*, Knopf, 1951.

MORGENTHAU, H. *Politics Among Nations*, Knopf, 1960.

*MORGENTHAU, H. *A New Foreign Policy for the United States*, Pall Mall Press, 1969.

*MORSE, E. 'The transformation of foreign policies', *World Politics*, xxii, no. 1, 371–92.

MORSE, E. *A Comparative Approach to the Study of Foreign Policy*, Research Monograph no. 36, Centre of International Studies, Princeton University, 1971.

MUNDELL, R. A. and SWOBODA, A. *Monetary Problems of the International Economy*, University of Chicago Press, 1969.

NETTL. J. 'The state as a conceptual variable', *World Politics*, xx, no. 4, 1968, 559–92.

NETTL, J. and ROBERTSON, R. *International Systems and the Modernisation of Societies* Faber, 1968.

NEUSTADT, R. *Alliance Politics*, Columbia University Press, 1970.

NICOLSON, H. *Diplomacy*, Oxford University Press, 1939.

NICOLSON, H. *The Evolution of Diplomatic Method*, Constable, 1954.

NORTHEDGE, F. S., ed. *The Foreign Policies of the Powers*, Faber, 1968.

*OSGOOD, R. *Alliances and American Foreign Policy*, Johns Hopkins Press, 1968.

PATEMAN, C. *Participation and Democratic Theory*, Cambridge University Press, 1970.

REYNOLDS, P. A. *An Introduction to International Relations*, Longman, 1971.

RICHARDS, J. *International Economic Institutions*, Holt, Rinehart & Winston, 1970.

RICHARDS, P. *Parliament and Foreign Affairs*, Allen & Unwin, 1967.

ROSECRANCE, R. *Action and Reaction in World Politics*, Little, 1963.

ROSECRANCE, R. *Defence of the Realm*, Columbia University Press, 1968.

*ROSENAU, J., ed. *Domestic Sources of Foreign Policy*, Collier-Macmillan, 1967.

*ROSENAU, J., ed. *Linkage Politics*, Collier-Macmillan, 1969.

*ROSENAU, J. *The Scientific Study of Foreign Policy*, Collier-Macmillan, 1971.

RUSSETT, B. *International Regions and the International System*, Rand McNally, New York, 1967.

RUSSETT, B., ed. *Economic Theories of International Politics*, Chicago, Markham Publishing Co., 1968.

SCHELLING, T. *The Strategy of Conflict*, Harvard University Press, 1963.

SCHUMPETER, J. *Capitalism, Socialism and Democracy*, Allen & Unwin, 1943.

SCOTT, A. *The Functioning of the International Political System*, Collier-Macmillan, 1967.

*SHONFIELD, A. *Europe: Journey to an Unknown Destination*, Penguin Books Pelican, 1973.

SHONFIELD, A. *Modern Capitalism*, Oxford University Press, 1965.

SHONFIELD, A. 'The Duncan Report and its critics', *International Affairs*, xlvi, no. 2, 1970, 247–68.

SINGER, M. *Weak States in a World of Powers*, Collier-Macmillan, 1972.

SNYDER, R., BRUCK, H. and SAPIN, B., eds. *Foreign Policy Decision Making*, Free Press, Glencoe, 1962.

SNYDER, W. *The Politics of British Defence Policy, 1945–62*, Ernest Benn, London, 1965.

SPIRO, H. *World Politics: the global system*, Homewood, Ill., Dorsay Press, 1966.

SPROUT, H. and SPROUT, M. *The Ecological Perspective on Human Affairs, with Special Reference to International Politics*, Princeton University Press, 1965.

SPROUT, H. and SPROUT, M. *Toward a Politics of the Planet Earth*, Van Nostrand Reinhold, 1971.

STEUER, M. *et al. The Impact of Foreign Direct Investment on the United Kingdom*, HMSO, 1973.

STRANG, W. *Britain in World Affairs*, Faber, 1961.

STRANGE, S. *Sterling and British Policy*, Oxford University Press, 1971.

*STRANGE, S. 'The politics of international currencies', *World Politics*, xxiii, 1971, 214–31.

STRANGE, S. 'The dollar crisis 1971', *International Affairs*, xlviii, no. 2, 1972, 191–215.

TAUTER, R. and ULLMAN, R., eds. *Theory and Policy in International Relations*, a special supplement of *World Politics*, xxiv, 1972.

TAYLOR, A. J. P. *The Trouble Makers: dissent over foreign policy, 1792–1939*, Hamish Hamilton, 1957.

TAYLOR, P. 'The functionalist approach to the problem of international order: a defence', *Political Studies*, xvi, 1968, 393–410.

TUGENDHAT, C. *The Multinationals*, Eyre & Spottiswoode, 1971.

URWIN, D. *Western Europe Since 1945*, Longman, 1968.

*VITAL, D. *The Making of British Foreign Policy*, Unwin, 1968.

WALLACE, W. *Foreign Policy and the Political Process*, Macmillan, 1971.

WALTZ, K. *Foreign Policy and Democratic Politics: the American and British Experience*, Longman, 1968.

*WALTZ, K. 'The myth of national interdependence', in Kindleberger, C., ed., *The International Corporation*, Massachusetts Institute of Technology, 1970, 205–23.

WATKINS, F. *The State as a Concept of Political Science*, Harper, 1934.

WATT, D. 'The Home Civil Service and the new diplomacy', *Political Quarterly*, xxxviii, 1967, 283–9.

WOLFERS, A., and MARTIN, L. *The Anglo-American Tradition in Foreign Affairs*, Yale University Press, 1956.

WOLFERS, A. *Alliance Policy in the Cold War*, Johns Hopkins Press, 1959.

*WOLFERS, A. *Discord and Collaboration*, Johns Hopkins Press, 1962.

YOUNG, O. *A Systemic Approach to International Politics*, Centre of International Studies, Princeton University, 1968, Research Monograph no. 33.

*YOUNG, O. 'Political discontinuities in the international system', *World Politics*, xx, no. 3, 1968, 369–92.

Index

Africa, 23, 29
alchemy, 10
alliances, 7, 17, 19, 23, 24, 40, 56, 58, 62, 76, 77, 81, 85, 86, 110, 123, 132, 155, 173
Antarctic, 27, 31
apathy, 154
appeasement, 41, 87
arms control, 31, 32, 33, 82, 85, 89, 167
arms race, 31, 34, 89, 90
Australia, 73, 128, 133
authority, 4, 18, 92, 118, 154
autonomy, 45, 46, 55, 92, 94, 96, 98, 99, 100, 101, 105, 113, 131, 181

balance of power, 11, 112, 125
banks, 37, 44, 102
Berlin, 82, 87
boundaries, 11, 22, 112
Brussels, 149, 152
bureaucracy, 2, 141, 145, 151, 166

capital, movements of, 9, 37, 43, 47, 49, 96, 113, 132, 151
Caribbean, 22
chambers of commerce, 169
chauvinism, 124
China, 12, 32, 52
coercion, 150
Cold War, 135
communications, 5, 152, 158
complementarity, 106, 107, 108, 118, 120, 139, 181
Concorde, 87
Confederation of British Industry, 149, 166

conflict, 21, 22, 23, 24, 29, 73, 117, 133, 156
consensus, 7, 12
convergence, 44
Cuba, 22
Czechoslovakia, 12

defence, 7, 17, 25, 26, 27, 28, 32, 40, 42, 48, 52, 53, 56, 64, 76, 77, 79, 80, 83, 87, 101, 108, 132, 136, 163
budgets, 31
and security, 33, 34, 75, 81, 82, 87, 90, 112
democracy, 40, 107, 128, 140–64
diplomacy, 6, 28, 35, 54, 55, 60, 62, 65, 156
transformation of, 55, 56, 63, 117, 119, 147, 157, 175
diplomatists, 119, 147, 153, 156, 166, 168
disarmament, 82
disease, 5
dollar, 36, 41, 46, 48, 51, 59, 61, 97, 99, 102, 104
as *numeraire*, 51

East Indies, 70
elections, 142, 144, 148
elites, 2, 128, 154, 155, 156, 157, 158
equality, 55
equilibrium, 158
Eurogroup, 86
Europe, 20, 22, 24, 26, 29, 32, 33, 52, 56, 63, 74, 75, 76, 78, 79, 80, 85, 86, 109, 118, 125

Europe—*cond*
  Eastern, 20, 29, 34, 84, 90, 101, 104, 115
  Western, 28, 34, 56, 72, 73, 77
  defence of, 28, 29, 30, 62, 75, 76, 78, 79, 80, 83, 85, 101, 104, 110, 111, 168
European Economic Community (EEC), 6, 47, 48, 49, 56, 59, 62, 63, 80, 90, 92, 95, 101, 102, 103, 107, 113, 129, 131, 142, 151, 152, 157, 159, 170
  Assembly (Parliament) of, 65, 98, 144, 174
  Commission of, 141, 144
  common agricultural policy of, 58, 61
  and common currency, 38, 42, 48, 49, 95, 99, 100, 105, 106
  Council of Ministers of, 65, 141, 144
  programme of, 8, 38, 49, 59, 74, 100
European security organisation, 89, 90, 91, 137

Far East, 41, 52
federalism, 153, 177
first-rank powers, 12, 17, 19, 20, 21, 22, 24, 27, 28, 31, 33, 35, 62, 71, 77, 79, 82, 85, 87, 90, 109, 110
flexible response, 24, 25, 26, 29, 81, 83, 84
foreign policy, *see under* Great Britain
France, 20, 32, 41, 42, 79, 81, 83, 90, 130, 176
free trade, 126, 151

General Agreement on Tariffs and Trade (GATT), 52, 58, 59, 61, 62, 64, 95, 104
Geneva, 82
geography, 17, 123, 126
Germany, 127
  Federal German Republic, 34, 42, 52, 61, 75, 78, 79, 80, 83, 87, 102, 103, 109, 134
  German Democratic Republic, 29, 78
gold, 36, 38, 40, 48, 128, 151

governments, as international actors, 13
Great Britain
  and balance of payments, 41, 42, 46, 47, 50, 92, 94, 98, 103, 106, 108, 109, 116, 138
  Cabinet of, 2, 145, 169, 170, 171, 176, 177
  and Commonwealth, 23, 65, 70, 110, 126, 129, 133, 134, 135
  decline of, 34, 109, 125–9, 131, 132, 133
  and defence, 23, 33, 47, 59, 70, 72, 73, 75, 76–83, 85, 87, 88, 90, 91, 101
  diplomatic service, 167, 168
  and EEC, 47, 49, 62, 65, 80, 94, 101, 103, 104, 107, 108, 117, 131, 141, 142, 145, 163, 174
  and Empire, 23, 46, 125, 126, 127, 155
  and Europe, 47, 75, 85, 86, 87, 91
  Foreign and Commonwealth Office of, 165–9
  and foreign investment, 39, 46, 47, 69, 94
  foreign policy of,
    transformations in, 1–10, 58, 111, 112, 113, 116, 117, 119, 130, 131, 132, 133, 136–8, 142, 143, 145, 167, 169, 170, 171, 173, 178, 179
    traditional, 1, 9, 10, 109, 110, 111, 116, 118, 119, 123–9, 135, 140, 142, 149, 155, 165, 167, 170, 171, 173–6, 178, 180
  Foreign Secretary of, 165, 171, 172
  House of Commons of, 2, 147, 171, 172, 173, 177
  proposed committee of foreign affairs of, 172
  Public Expenditure Committee of, 174
  ministerial responsibility, 145
  Ministry of Defence of, 165
  nationalised industries, 168
  Prime Minister of, 165, 167, 171
  and security, 34, 59, 82, 88, 89, 91, 111

and sterling, 46, 47, 93, 103, 104, 110, 126, 127, 128, 129, 130, 133
and Suez expedition, 23
trade of, 39, 46, 94, 126
and underdeveloped countries, 23, 65, 70, 71, 72, 73, 74
and United States, 34, 62, 69, 70, 73, 81, 83, 85, 86, 91, 96, 101, 106, 108, 109, 110, 126, 128, 129
Whitehall, 167–9
Greece, 176

Hayek, F. A., 150 fn.
Hitler, A., 146
Hungary, 20

Iceland, 177
incrementalism, 161–3
India, 21, 73, 127
Indian Ocean, 23, 70, 73
Indian subcontinent, 20
Indo-China, 70
Industrial Revolution, 127
inflation, 50, 106
influence, 2, 123, 157
interdependence, 38, 39, 42, 43, 45, 53, 96, 97, 101, 102, 161, 163, 175
international assemblies, 6, 174, 175
international economy, 4, 35, 36, 38, 42, 43, 51, 56, 93, 94, 95, 97, 98, 99, 101, 102, 103, 107, 113, 135, 159
and national power, 38, 39, 40, 41, 42, 98
International Monetary Fund (IMF), 36, 38, 45, 48, 49, 50, 51, 59, 61, 62, 63, 95, 98, 102, 104, 105, 107, 113, 134, 159
and fixed exchange rates, 41, 42, 44, 50, 51
Special Drawing Rights (SDRs), 38, 42, 48, 64, 93, 97, 104, 105
international organisation, 6, 18, 32, 33, 63, 64, 75, 152
international relations, character of, 3–5, 10, 11, 12, 20
discontinuities in, 12, 21, 35, 36
intervention, 19, 21, 23, 70, 113

Italy, 79

Japan, 19, 32, 39, 47, 51, 52, 53, 61, 72, 73, 126, 127, 134

Korea, 20

League of Nations, 18, 56, 155
legal orders, domestic and international, 4
legislative process, 5, 173–4
legitimacy, 19, 124
liberty, 150–2, 162
local authorities, 147
London, 126
Low Countries, 126

Malaya, 134
Malta, 171
markets, international, 6, 10, 36, 97
eurodollar, 37, 40, 43, 58, 97
massive retaliation, 24, 84
Mediterranean, 171
methodology, 179
Middle East, 20, 27, 42, 71
mobilisation, 126–7
models, 11
monopolies, 44, 131, 138
morality, 9, 176
multinational companies, 12, 36, 37, 58, 59, 96, 131, 160, 169
Munich, 8

national interest, 7, 8, 17, 33, 50, 116, 180
nationalism, 19
negotiation, from strength, 29
New Zealand, 73, 128
North Atlantic Treaty Organisation (Nato), 6, 23, 24, 34, 56, 64, 78, 79, 80, 81, 82–5, 89, 90, 96, 112, 148, 173
Norway, 79
nuclear deterrence, 3, 4, 11, 12, 17, 21, 22, 24, 29, 30, 35, 41, 75, 76, 81, 83, 87, 91
credibility of, 27, 81, 83, 84, 85
graduated, 24, 25, 27, 84

nuclear deterrence—*contd*
  instability of, 26, 30, 82
nuclear non-proliferation treaty, 32

oil, 42, 53, 94, 105, 111, 114, 127, 130
  producers of, 12, 37, 115, 132
Organisation for Economic Cooperation and Development, 166

Pakistan, 21, 73
partial test-ban treaty, 31
participation, 145–9
peace, 114, 134, 146
Persian Gulf, 23, 70
pluralism, 5, 7, 8, 159–60
political behaviour, 153
political parties, 6, 147, 158, 175
power, 2, 38, 54, 60, 61, 123–39, 163
  omissions of, 133–5
  irrelevance of, 135–8
  see also strength
public expenditure, 6, 174

radio, 5
rationality, 162
referenda, 148, 149
religion, 57, 58
representation, 142, 144, 145
Rhodesia, 155
Rome, 19

science, 12, 57
Scotland, 138
sea power, 22, 30, 72, 85, 125
second-class powers, 3, 19, 34, 46, 47,
  56, 78, 87
security, 17, 18, 31, 32, 63, 76, 77, 79,
  88
  see also defence
Singapore, 23
social justice, 55
  policies, 43
South Africa, 48, 176
South-east Asia, 70
sovereignty, 17, 38, 40, 45, 57, 58, 59,
  60, 76, 91, 92, 94, 96, 98, 99,
  100, 105, 111, 113, 118, 120,
  135, 156, 175, 181
speculation, 9, 47, 49

state, 1, 2, 39, 54, 57, 58, 59, 60, 73, 76,
  119, 123, 132
  and defence, 6, 7, 17
  dominance of, 8, 9, 12, 13
  permeability and impermeability of,
    5, 6, 7, 9, 13, 20, 38, 39, 45, 55
  static nature of, 9
statecraft, 9, 35, 57, 154, 160, 167
status quo, 71, 81, 87, 109, 118
sterling, *see under* Great Britain
strength,
  economic, 38, 40, 41, 52, 60, 61
  military, 3, 4, 18, 19, 20, 21, 26, 29,
    30, 33, 56, 70, 72, 73, 76, 80, 82,
    83, 163
  sources of, 123–6, 136
subversion, 22
suffrage, 35
systems, 5, 10, 12, 25, 26, 31, 32, 36, 38,
  41, 46, 52, 57, 60, 71, 75, 89,
  107, 117, 120, 132, 148, 180
  systemic control, 57, 58, 59, 60

taxation, 43, 44, 93, 96, 132, 160
technology, 27, 28, 32
trade unions, 4, 6, 57, 166
transnational organisations, 34, 37, 38,
  56, 58, 59, 60, 61, 62, 104, 105,
  106, 107, 108, 112, 113, 117,
  131, 133, 137, 152, 169, 177, 180
  relations, 55, 57, 58, 59, 60, 65, 93,
    96, 131, 132, 170, 176, 178, 179
treaties, 30, 31, 32, 79, 98, 127
tripwire, 26
tyranny, 18

underdeveloped countries, 23, 65, 70,
  71, 72, 104, 133
Union of Soviet Socialist Republics
  (USSR), 3, 20, 28, 29, 30, 31,
  48, 52, 61, 71, 72, 73, 75, 78, 79,
  82, 83, 85, 86, 87, 89, 110, 128,
  170
United Nations Organisation, 18, 32,
  63, 64, 75, 155
  military staff committee of, 33
  Security Council, 33
  small states and, 33, 63

United States, 3, 20, 29, 36, 37, 61, 64,
73, 78, 80, 87, 96, 102, 104, 106,
107, 126, 130, 151, 167, 180
commitment to allies, 22, 24, 26, 28,
29, 30, 31, 34, 58
Congress, 61
and EEC, 61, 63, 64, 100, 101
imperialism of, 62
and international economic system,
12, 36, 39, 40, 41–3, 46, 50–2, 62
and multinational companies, 36, 37,
40, 46
and postwar order, 60, 62
strategy of, 24, 26, 28, 31, 40, 58, 61,
83, 84, 85, 86
strength of, 39, 40, 41, 43, 46, 48, 52,
60, 61
and USSR, 28, 29, 30, 31, 52, 61, 89,
109
and Western Europe, 28, 30, 33, 41,
80, 84, 86, 89, 98, 110

Vietnam, 20, 29, 31, 41, 173

Wales, 138
war, 3, 24, 33, 35, 54, 55, 56, 57, 114,
134, 151
limited, 25
first world, 39
second world, 19, 37, 40, 46, 57, 60,
128
sublimited, 19
Warsaw Pact, 32, 34, 82
weapons,
conventional, 26, 29, 61, 84
nuclear, 6, 20, 21, 22, 24, 27, 29, 55,
63, 77, 78, 84, 85, 91
instability of, 30
rationality and, 25
strategic, 25, 26
tactical, 25, 26, 83
testing, 31
world order, 17, 18, 73
world society, 54, 57, 59, 62, 153, 156

zealots, 148